INSIDE THE TRANSFORMATIVE WORLD OF CHILDREN'S MINISTRY

KYLE TYLER

f

THE FOUNDRY
PUBLISHING

Copyright © 2018 by The Foundry Publishing
The Foundry Publishing
PO Box 419527
Kansas City, MO 64141
thefoundrypublishing.com

978-0-8341-3749-3

All rights reserved. No part of this publication may be reproduced, stored in a retrieval system, or transmitted in any form or by any means—for example, electronic, photocopy, recording—without the prior written permission of the publisher. The only exception is brief quotations in printed reviews.

Cover Designer: Sherwin Schwartzrock
Interior Designer: Sharon Page

Library of Congress Cataloging-in-Publication Data
A complete catalog record for this book is available from the Library of Congress.

The internet addresses, email addresses, and phone numbers in this book are accurate at the time of publication. They are provided as a resource. The Foundry Publishing does not endorse them or vouch for their content or permanence.

Praise for *Inside the Transformative World of Children's Ministry*

"Any lead pastor who claims to believe in children's ministry needs to study this book. Kyle Tyler articulates a vision for children's ministry in the local church that is very different from what many of our congregations experience. Tyler's vision is theologically robust and educationally sound; it provides a philosophical framework from which healthy and sustainable Christian formation can happen in intergenerational communities of faith. Pastors and congregations with the countercultural courage to implement this vision will enjoy the fruit of thoroughly Christian and Wesleyan discipleship that forms people in the way of Jesus. I recommend this thoughtful and practical resource."

Rev. Jeren Rowell, Ed.D.
President and Professor
Nazarene Theological Seminary

"Kyle Tyler combines his years of experience in children's ministry with his theological and biblical training to present a book that is practical and theologically solid. Children's ministry needs a voice that understands the complexities of leading ministry with children while not forgetting the importance of providing ministry that transforms children into the image of Christ. This book provides sound and practical advice for all children's ministry leaders. I am thankful for such a solid resource, which I will use in my Foundations of Children's Ministry class."

Rev. Leon Blanchette, Ed.D.
Chair, Department of Christian Ministry
Chair, School of Theology and Christian Ministry
Olivet Nazarene University

For my mother, my first children's pastor.

And for my wife, my partner in ministry always and crime when necessary.

CONTENTS

Foreword	7
Introduction	11
1. Why It Matters	17
2. Value the Role	31
3. Training	59
4. Volunteers	77
5. Intergenerational Ministry	93
6. A Safe Place	115
7. Make Space	129
8. Hiring a Children's Leader	143
Notes	155
Acknowledgments	157

FOREWORD

I needed this book a few decades ago. And I think I may finally be old enough to write the foreword to it. Why? Time has proven to me that the longest and deepest impact of my pastoral ministry resides in the memories of the children who caught the culture of the church while we adults were busy running its programs.

Our most effective evangelism is to infect children with our love of Jesus. I think senior pastors, church boards, and leaders need to get their arms around this reality. Our love for immediate success in adult conversion and instant church growth has given us a distaste for a field of seedling oaks. We prefer the grown "show-and-tell mighty oak" to hundreds of little acorns sprouting toward a future that will unfold well after we are gone. Over time, the best chance of having strong churches in the next generation is to invest in the newest generation among us. And this is hard work.

For all these reasons and more, I am glad that Kyle has written this book. He is realistic, humorous, non-stuffy, and passionate. He lives what he has written and is fulfilling a call to help us all do ministry among and with children better than we currently are.

I commend several things to your attention. Catch his spirit. Children need a specific culture more than they need a program that adults pat themselves on the back for launching. This culture values children and their families. It listens to them, prepares to serve them, and organizes the social life of the church to include them. It needs trained volunteers who are also highly valued and supported. It needs a senior pastor who knows how to view children as key congregational constituents, not noisy little ones who need to be entertained while the adults do their thing. It needs a safe environment, space to function, and a budget that reflects the value of children. It needs an intergenerational footprint that has lots of people who know the whole family, or single-parent families who believe they have been graced with an extended family via the church. And it needs a team of leaders working together, not in silos, for the good of the children.

If these issues are important to you, you have found your book. Kyle will walk us through the practical challenges and rewards of doing children's ministry well.

I received an email recently from a child I baptized sixteen years ago. She was planning a college visit where I now serve as president, five hundred miles from her home.

"Why would you be interested in Trevecca in Nashville?" I asked.

Her answer humbled and surprised me. "The way I felt in the church when I was a child made me think that maybe it was your leadership that created the kind of culture that made people feel valued, loved, and bettered. I'm taking a chance that you're still doing that where you are now."

An acorn turned into an oak. I plan to enjoy the shade of another tall tree in the making.

Dan Boone
President
Trevecca Nazarene University

INTRODUCTION

Along with phenomenal colleagues, from whom I've learned much, I've been privileged to host children's pastors at leadership conferences across the U.S. Part of my role in these hosting gigs is making everyone laugh, and there are no shortage of children's pastor jokes to be made. We rib, good-naturedly, other pastors and pick the church apart in ways that only people who deeply love the church can. We make fun of the hardships of children's ministry and the daily grind of the children's pastor. My friend and I have written song parodies that are all about the struggle of the children's pastor, including plenty of self-deprecation and stereotypes of the role.

We wrote "You Make Everything Difficult" to the tune of "You Make Everything Glorious," a worship song made popular by David Crowder. Our parody is written to Sunday school curriculum writers about the ways they make a children's leader's life so hard with all of the supplies we have to collect just to teach a Sunday school lesson. It's not uncommon to open a leader's guide and see that you have to make homemade pudding, gather some dry garbanzo beans, cut fourteen different shapes from construction paper, have a myriad of chenille stems available (that's what pipe cleaners are called now . . . did you know?), and pick through animal crackers until you have two by two of every available beast.

☀ Children's leaders are a different breed.

Have you ever taken a group of preteens to a restaurant? We wrote another song, "Finish Your Fries," to parody Brandon Heath's contemporary Christian hit "Give Me Your Eyes." His song is about seeing the world through Jesus's eyes. This is much more respectable than our song, which is about taking preteens to McDonald's. If you've never taken a large group of eleven-year-olds out in public, do it so you can identify with Jesus in the wilderness—except that your temptation will be to drive off and leave everybody there. Usually, you are working within a budget and the kids need to order within a certain dollar amount. Sometimes they each have their own money, but they're so used to their parents ordering for them that they ask you to explain things on the menu. You're like, "It's a chicken sandwich. Mayo. Lettuce. Yes, it comes with fries, but only if you get the value meal. No, they don't serve tacos. No, I don't think Big Macs are gluten-free. Kids, remember, Sprite only! No caffeine!" It's stressful. Then you manage the spills and the noise level and the bathroom breaks, all while your own McNuggets get cold.

Yes, I'm overstating. But there's some truth underneath. My colleagues and I write these songs and do these bits at conferences so the children's leaders can all laugh together at our crazy lives. We get each other. We've all been there with the pudding and animal crackers. We've all been there with the preteens and extra pickles on their burgers. Children's leaders are a different breed. It's nice to be with our own.

The different nature of the children's pastor's job propelled me to write this book. I've been a children's pastor for more than a decade now. Recently, I've moved into a role of training and support, helping to equip other staffs and children's leadership teams. I've been on staffs of varying sizes, seen budgets of varying dollars, faced ecclesiologies of varying degrees of similarity to my own, and come to a simple realization: sometimes church leaders (pastors, board members, etc.) really aren't sure what to do with children's ministry.

Ministering to kids can be overwhelming. I get it. Most senior pastors don't come from a professional children's ministries background. There are the exceptions, of course, but purely from anecdotal evidence it would seem that more lead pastors start their vocational ministry with youth, worship, or discipleship than with children's ministry. Really, the idea of vocational children's ministry is a relatively young phenomenon, in the church world anyway. Simply put, children's ministry has not been in a lot of lead pastors' wheelhouses, and they have relied heavily on either the experts, or volunteer moms and dads, to lead in that area.

What if you are a local church leader without an expert? Or what if you and your children's ministry expert are struggling to get on the same page? Or what if you've gotten to the place where you're ready to hire an expert and you want to make an informed decision? This book is for you.

Inside the Transformative World of Children's Ministry is for lead pastors, executive pastors, church boards, deacons, and other leaders in the church who are seeking insider knowledge on ministry to children, and perhaps a better understanding of the person or people who lead that ministry. This book will take you into the life of a children's leader, be it a director, pastor, or volunteer. We'll explore what children's leaders hold dear and how you can best support and partner with them. We'll open up the kid-min contraption to see the gears turning and figure out what's turning them. Sometimes we'll examine the vocation of children's ministry at a philosophical, bird's-eye view. At other times, we'll wander a little further into the weeds of ministry.

Our children's ministry leadership team at The Foundry Kids surveyed children's leaders from across the U.S. who serve in varying church sizes and who hold various positions. The survey included only people who were "in charge" of children's ministry at their churches. This was mostly made up of full-time children's pastors, part-time children's pastors, full- or part-time children's directors, and volunteer children's directors. We'll refer to the whole group throughout this book as children's leaders. Obviously, a church has to be a certain size to afford salaries for full-time staff members, so it's likely those full-timers represent churches of over two hundred. It's often our smaller churches that can't pay a professional children's leader, so the volunteer directors are typically representing that sub-one hundred demographic. These are often very involved parents who saw a need and stepped up to fill it. One day they were volunteering to teach Sunday school in their kid's class, the next they find themselves in charge of children's ministry for the whole church. They are not trained professionals in the world of ministry to kids, but they are still passionate about seeing children's ministry thrive!

I'll reference the aforementioned Children's Leadership Survey throughout this book. The questions were often open-ended and provided excellent insight to what sort of support children's leaders need from their church leadership. They were able to speak freely about their education, their wins, their losses, where they saw communication breaking down, when they felt valued, and when they felt forgotten.

If you're looking to add intentionality to your children's ministry, *Inside the Transformative World of Children's Ministry* will help you have a shared language and speak from a place of empathy as you address the issues at hand. I'm interested in spurring churches to a stronger culture of ministry to kids and families. I'm interested in shaping relationships between children's leaders and church leadership. I'm interested in offering the tools to equip and empower a children's leader to be the best he or she can be. I'm interested in the church raising kids who stick around. I want staff relationships to deepen, volunteer needs to crystallize, and ministries to grow. If you share these same goals, keep reading! Perhaps by the end of this short book, children's leaders and other church leadership will be laughing at the same jokes because you're all insiders now. You get it. Let's see what makes those gears turn. Finish your fries. I'll try not to make everything difficult. Let's jump in.

✺ 1 ✺
WHY IT MATTERS

One evening I sat in a church board meeting before it began, quietly surveying the people in the room. There was a young dad of three who owned his own construction business, a highly educated and well-spoken school administrator, a retired coach, a stay-at-home mom, a nurse, a salesperson, and our pastors. I was preparing to present the good, bad, and ugly of children's ministry in our church. We would talk about parent involvement, volunteer recruitment, children's baptism, how Sundays and Wednesdays were going, etc. I had a report prepared, but something struck me as I looked around the room. I began to wonder about the personal testimonies of the people sitting at the table. So, when my turn came, I asked a simple question before diving into my report. "How many of you had a significant encounter with Jesus before the age of twelve?" All but two people raised their hands. I knew I was on to something.

George Barna conducted a series of studies regarding the age at which people accept Christ as their Savior. In his research, he noted a startling statistic. The chance of someone embracing Jesus as their

Savior is 32% before the age of twelve. That chance drops to just 4% in the teenage years, and raises to 6% for those nineteen and older. Barna writes, "In other words, if people do not embrace Jesus Christ as their Savior before they reach their teenage years, the chance of their doing so at all is slim."[1] I had this statistic in mind when I asked the church board members to raise their hands. Their participation seemed to validate Barna's research.

These statistics are why children's ministry matters. A person will never be so likely to embrace Jesus as he or she will in the formative years. Hope isn't lost at the age of thirteen, but the battle certainly begins to turn uphill. Children are naturally inclined to believe. Faith is not an intellectual struggle the way it is with many adults. Love is not something that has to be taught.

When my wife and I first became parents, we were thrilled. We were also scared. We had enjoyed our nieces and nephews, but we always sent them home at the end of the day. We were just the fun aunt and uncle, not the people in charge of their lives. The very first night alone in our own house with our own baby, we quickly came to grips with the reality that we had to not only keep this little one alive but we also had to help her thrive and flourish. My wife was an educator, and I was a children's pastor, but we had no real idea how to take care of our *own* baby. Somehow, like most parents do, we figured it out.

I remember looking down in the crib at my little baby daughter, thinking of all the things I was going to teach her to do. I would teach her how to swing a golf club, how to play guitar, and how to catch a baseball. I picked her up and changed her diaper. I sang to her. I read her a book. I played on the floor with her. There would be time for her to learn all those things, but for now it was just good to be in her presence. I adored her.

Our routine went on. My wife and I cared for her, keeping her fed, bathed, and warm. We doted on her, kissed her face about a billion times, and tended to her every need.

As she got older, there were certain things we definitely had to teach her. We had to give her tools to learn to walk, to potty train, to hold a fork, and to hold her little sister. Eventually, I began teaching her music and baseball as well.

One thing I realized, though, that we never had to teach her, was that she loved us. We didn't teach her love. We didn't have long sessions of working on love over and over at the table until we got it right. She caught on to love by being loved. I didn't have to show her a picture of my wife in a book and remind her that we are to always love our mommy. She picked that up on her own. She was born into love and was naturally inclined to love.

The same went for her love for Jesus. She heard about Jesus from day one as we prayed with her. Jesus was central in our household. We gave him praise together every day. My wife and I loved Jesus. Naturally, our daughter picked up on that as well. We have to teach Scripture. We have to teach theology. We don't have to teach love. We show love. Loving Jesus comes more naturally for children because their worldview is still being formed.

As children develop socially, cognitively, and emotionally, they develop spiritually. Catherine Stonehouse, seminary professor and expert on children's spirituality, writes, "In the process of development there comes a right time for learning certain lessons at the unconscious, feeling levels. Because of this, persons are drawn to specific theological ideas at particular stages in human development." In the earliest days of a child's life, this theological idea is as simple as, "God loves me. I love God." By allowing them to live in this truth daily, it can become reality.[2]

Simone Biles was nineteen years old when she won four gold medals for the U.S. Olympic team in Rio de Janeiro. At the time, her name, face, and accomplishments were omnipresent. She set records in gymnastics, and she was a lot of fun to watch and cheer for. Commentators compared her to Michael Jordan, Michael Phelps, and Tiger Woods, all athletes who dominated their respective sports in their prime. Just like those other athletes, Biles started training at a young age. Her parents recall her as a young girl always climbing and jumping, rambunctious and full of life. She discovered gymnastics at six years of age on a daycare field trip. It wasn't long before she was training with a coach. Less than five years later, she was ranked at the top level of the Junior Olympic system.[3] The rest of the story, as they say, is history.

What if Simone's parents had waited to put her in gymnastics when it was closer to time for her to compete in the Olympics? What if they had said, "Well, you might show some promise, but the 2016 Olympics is more than ten years from now. We'll get you going a little closer to time!" What if they had recognized that she had some skills, so they put her in a fun gymnastics class so she could run around and play in a gymnastics environment with other little girls? What if they had decided that was sufficient? Would Simone's life have been a terrible one? Probably not. Would she be the Simone Biles the world knows? Definitely not. Not only did it take her parents recognizing the opportunity they had to get Simone some real, high-quality training, but it took her parents, trainers, and friends sticking by her as she put in the work for all those years.

Let's jump over to the church. Imagine we said to our kids, "We'll get your training started, but you won't need the strong theology or a grasp on hermeneutics until you're older, so we'll wait a bit. Instead, we'll put you in a pleasant, church-centered environment so you can hang out with your friends and do church-related things. That'll be fun, right?"

Sure, our kids would be good with that arrangement. They would love to play, maybe watch a video with some talking vegetables that teach a nice moral, and eat some snacks. But we can fast-forward to adulthood and see where this lack of planning and investment takes us. We're left with young adults who have lots of spiritual questions but no tools to use in their search. We're left with young adults who might have all the books of the Bible memorized but no grasp on how to understand or apply it. We're left with young adults who love the church for social reasons, but when things get tough, or relationships get thin, they turn to other social outlets instead.

If our goal as church leaders is to nurture spiritually mature, strong, world-changing adults, it begins with orthodox teaching *by* spiritually mature, strong, world-changing adults *to* our kids. And our kids are ready for this kind of teaching.

> ☀ **A child who has never heard of Jesus won't scoff and roll her eyes like an adult might. Rather, she's more likely to believe in even the most supernatural parts of the story because believing comes much more naturally to kids.**

Kids are comfortable learning about God because mystery doesn't scare them. Instead, it inspires wonder. The world around them is full of mystery. It's a part of life. Not only are they not afraid of it, but they're drawn to it. In *Opening Your Child's Spiritual Windows*, Cheri Fuller talks about the wonder window. She quotes Miriam Rockness, author of several works on home, family, and faith. Rockness says, "Wonder, amazement, awe—such are the characteristic signatures of childhood. Children, novice to their ever-changing world, are alert, aware and alive to the natural bounty constantly being revealed."[4] When a child hears about the Red Sea parting for the first time, he's less likely to say, "That's impossible!" and more likely to say, "Whoa! Really? Cool!" A child who has never heard of Jesus won't scoff and roll her eyes like an adult might. Rather, she's more likely to believe in even the most supernatural parts of the story because believing comes much more naturally to kids.

We have a window of opportunity to help children embrace a giant, mysterious God. The four to fourteen window is a popular age range often cited in the world of children's ministry. However, I would contend that starting at four misses too many opportunities when children are babies and toddlers. Barna talks about this: "Physicians assert that children begin to absorb values as early as two years of age . . . Starting the developmental process when children are young is a reflection of the underlying philosophy: Because this is part of a spiritual battle, the longer you wait to pursue influence, the more difficult it is to counteract the influence of other parties that have been imprinting their values upon children."[5]

Absorbing values may begin at two years, but laying the foundation of love and trust begins at infancy. So don't be fooled by the four to fourteen window. Back that age four up to first breath. And, if you believe God goes before us, working preveniently in our lives, back it up to the prayers offered as soon as a little life is conceived (or whenever prayers for that life began). Faith questions will come, but capitalizing on this window to help kids know God, enjoy God, and embrace God even in the mystery will help them ask those questions with hearts and minds that have foundations rooted in faith.

In addition to being able to embrace mystery and catch on to love, children are also really good at loving. We may not take the time to teach them the word "soteriology," or explain the Trinitarian heresies that they should avoid in sound theology, but we can teach them about God's love for them. We can teach them how to respond to God's love and how to extend it to their neighbors. James K. A. Smith, professor of congregational and ministry studies at Calvin College, asks, "What if education (in the church) wasn't first and foremost about what we know, but about what we love?"[6] I'm suggesting that if an eight-year-old child was polled in our church's children's ministry and didn't have the books of the Bible memorized, couldn't recite Psalm 23 from heart, and perhaps had never even heard the story of Jonah, but she was certain God loved her and she knew beyond a shadow of a doubt that she loved him back, we would be on the right track! We would be establishing deep, relational concepts that she would be more likely to carry with her than if she was first discovering them just then at eight, or a couple years later in her early adolescent years.

I believe our churches' ministries to kids should resemble the deliberate coaching that Simone Biles received on her journey toward Olympic gold. She got excited about gymnastics in a fun introductory class, but she wasn't left in that kind of class for the rest of her formative years. She was put in a position to succeed because she had adults around her who were willing to embrace her natural abilities and help her hone them. Our kids have natural abilities to love and believe. Show value to your church's ministry to children by making it a priority to cultivate those abilities! To make such a commitment will require that your children's leaders have proper training. It will take the participation of your whole team to take this ministry to a deeper, more intentional level. Church leaders, spend some time with your children's leaders, observe ministry in action, and talk to them about how children's ministry can improve in your context. Together, you can bring up Christians who have for years experienced a rich relationship with a loving God, even before they know all the answers. Because our faith is first about who we know rather than what we know, in this way we would be establishing firm faith foundations upon which they could build mature and fruitful relationships with God. Could we raise a generation of Olympians?

☀ **Saying things like, "These kids are the church of the future" actually communicates that kids are still learning to be real Christians. Kids are the church of today because they are Christians, just like you and me, today.**

NOT JUST TRAINING

So far, we have been talking about children's ministry in terms of *training*, but it is important to make a distinction between *training* and *being*.

When Simone Biles was nine years old and training with a coach for a seemingly unreasonable number of hours each week, she was not yet an Olympic gymnast. But she was a gymnast.

Our children may have a lot to learn about what it means to be Christian, but that doesn't mean they're only *in training* to be Christians. They can *be* Christians right now. Being Christian is not a collection of things we know; being Christian is defined by our relationship with Jesus. Do you recognize God's love for you as your Savior, your King, and your Friend? Do you love him back as your Savior, your King, and your Friend? Then you are a Christian!

Saying things like, "These kids are the church of the future," while said with a good heart, actually communicates that kids are still learning to be real Christians. Kids are the church of today because they are Christians, just like you and me, today.

Consider the journey of faith. A first grader who has recently committed his life to Christ is on the same journey as the saint in your church in her seventieth year of following Jesus. She's much further along in her journey, but they're both walking the path. When we think and talk about our kids, let's use the language of present rather than future. Kids have trouble living for the future. It feels really far away when your entire life has only been seven years. By our words and actions, we can give them confidence to live in the present knowing they are Christians and very much a part of the church today.

A practical way to communicate to our children that they are important is to begin listening for stories of kids in your church who are doing things that are uniquely Christian. They don't have to be huge things. Put feelers out to some parents and children's leaders, asking them to bring you stories of kids helping neighbors, living an active prayer life, or inviting friends to church. When you hear such a story, find a way to highlight it to your congregation. Include it in the pastor's sermon, interview the child in the service, or feature a story on your website. Be sure people know it's a real child from within your congregation. Children can be wonderful sermon illustrations for living an incarnational Christian life! This will communicate significant value (1) to the kids in your church, (2) to your children's leaders, and (3) to the other adults in your church about the way you view children and children's ministry.

If being Christian is about what one knows, kids are just in training. If being Christian is about *who* one knows, kids can be Christians right now! Kids are a vital part of the church—right now.

THE FUTURE

I promise I'm not talking out of both sides of my mouth. I realize I invited you to invest in training kids, then I pointed out to you that training for the future isn't all we're doing. I believe strongly in involving kids in the present life of the church. Now I'm going to point us toward the future for a moment. It all works together.

Children's ministry matters not only for the present and future of the young Christians in your church, but for the future of your church and *the* Church (as in holy catholic). That's not news to you. You know your church won't last forever if young people aren't reached. What is your congregation actively doing to reach young families? Might I suggest an investment in children's ministry?

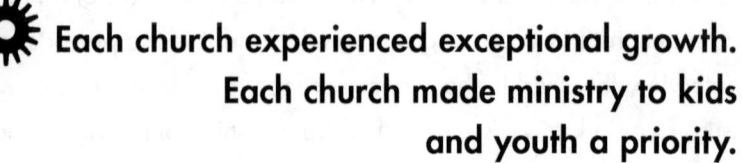 **Each church experienced exceptional growth. Each church made ministry to kids and youth a priority.**

Gallup polled adults across the U.S. to ask what appeals most to churchgoers. The top two poll answers had to do with sermons that (1) taught about Scripture and (2) were applicable to life. The third most popular answer among Protestants was "Spiritual programs geared toward children and teenagers."[7] This response was the second most popular option among Catholics. According to the survey, effective sermons and a robust ministry to children/youth should be getting the most of our attention.

A study was done within one Wesleyan denomination looking for churches that stood out from others in terms of growth. Specifically, nine churches made the cut for the study. Each of these churches studied began with an average worship attendance of fewer than one hundred persons and grew at a percentage rate double the average of their peers. Based on the study, a book was produced called *Shift: How Nine Churches Experienced Vibrant Renewal*. While there were several commonalities found in these churches as they grew, one specifically points to the subject at hand: "As vibrant pastors submitted to a three-year process of surveys and summits, one specific aspect of disciple-making became clear. All nine made a priority of making disciples of children and teenagers."[8] These churches focused on giving kids opportunities to serve, discipling kids as young as nursery age, and equipping parents to better disciple their own kids at home. Each church experienced exceptional growth. Each church made ministry to kids and youth a priority.

I like to joke with people that my mom is the first person I ever converted to Christianity. I was two weeks old. Impressive, I know. Though raised in a Christian home, my mom had moved away from any relationship with Jesus in her teenage years after her parents' divorce. She found a life of sin, met my dad who lived the same kind of life, and got married. In a few years, they decided to have a baby. Fast-forward several months and my mom is introducing her brand-new baby boy to her family. My uncle, my mom's younger brother, was a fresh-faced young minister and offered my mom a piece of advice. She has told the story many times, so I have no trouble recalling his words. "The best thing you can do for that baby is to raise him for Jesus." Soon after, my mom found herself at the altar rededicating her life to Christ.

It was her desire to see her baby raised right that brought my mom back to the church. According to the Gallup survey results, chances are there are several people sitting in your congregation who care a great deal about your church's ministry to their children. Your church is more than just a nice place to drop the kids off—children's ministry might be why they're sitting in the pews. It might even be what brought them to church, or back to church, in the first place, much like my mom's story. Simply put, a strong children's ministry can grow the church.

For me, this is the gear that turns all the others. This whole conversation is worth having because children's ministry matters. It's the present. It's the future. It's our best chance at helping to establish a lifelong relationship with Jesus. Every "how" that we approach from here on in will be driven by the "why" established in this chapter.

✺ 2 ✺
VALUE THE ROLE
(A Note to Lead Pastors)

In one city where there is a dense population of churches in my denomination, I found a strange phenomenon. There's a triangle of churches within two miles of each other. One church sees thousands come through their doors for worship each Sunday. One church sees a couple hundred. One church sees eighty to ninety. All three of these churches are in the same area of town but obviously have different ministry needs based on their size. One church employs multiple full-time children's pastors. One church employs a single, part-time children's pastor. One church has recruited a lay volunteer to lead children's ministry. Though these situations are very different, each children's ministry leader has something in common: they need to feel valued by their church leadership.

An educated, trained, full-time children's pastor might need different kinds of support from church leadership than does a mom at a small church who backed into the volunteer position to fill a void. Either way, let's consider how value can be shown to the ministry and the person leading it.

I'm not a lead pastor, nor have I been. I have spent my career both in the local church as a staff pastor in children's ministry, and in a broader role helping to equip other pastors to minister to kids and families. In this chapter, allow me to speak to senior pastors (or other church leaders, executives, board members, deacons, etc.) from the perspective of the children's leader.

MINE VS. OURS

Every pastor has a basic philosophy of staff ministry. The following concepts could apply not only to a relationship with a children's ministry leader, but with any staff members, both paid and volunteer. For ease, let's call one end of the spectrum *my ministry* and the other end *our ministry*. I'll offer a quick profile from different points on the spectrum to illustrate what children's staff may be perceiving about how their roles intersect with a pastor's style of leading. Every pastor is on this spectrum. Most pastors I know fall somewhere in the middle.

Pastor Steve leads from close to the *my ministry* end of the spectrum. He has what one might call a "top-down" idea of leadership. Steve is senior pastor, CEO, and president of his church. At board meetings, Steve does more talking than anyone else. Each area of ministry that reports begins and ends with Steve's involvement, even if Steve isn't involved on a daily or weekly basis with that ministry. On the back of the bulletin, Steve's name is listed first, above the rest of the pastoral staff, in big bold letters. Everyone else's name is down a font size or two and listed below Pastor Steve. The associate staff members don't experience a lot of ownership of their role or the church's vision as a whole. The vision wasn't crafted by the staff, but by Steve. Steve worked on the mission statement, laboring over it for hours and days in his own office until he had it just right, then he presented it to the staff as a finished product. They don't feel like they have a lot of room to push back on Steve's ideas, because he's the boss. Steve makes executive decisions often. Steve likes to be right. Steve preaches every Sunday except for his vacation weeks. Certain staff members are allowed to cover those, or Steve will choose pulpit-fill from a nearby university.

Pastor Charlotte leads from further down on the *our ministry* end of the spectrum. She is always giving away credit and responsibilities. She doesn't feel the need to micromanage each of the church's ministries, because she has put people she trusts into positions of leadership and allows them to lead. She's involved with various ministries not because she needs to be in charge, but because she makes herself available as a resource. She is glad to serve in the same role as any volunteer in activities for which she does not hold a direct leadership position. Pastor Charlotte's name is listed alphabetically on the back of the bulletin along with the other pastors, in the same font and size. She wants to communicate to anyone who reads the page that all of the staff are considered pastors and, though one is designated the leader, they are unranked. The church has a vision and mission statement that the staff crafted together in a series of meetings. They each feel comfortable pushing back on Charlotte's ideas because she has proven willing to listen. She is more interested in arriving at the right conclusion than she is being the one with the right answer. The staff also feels known and heard in the church as they are each given opportunities to preach throughout the year, even when Pastor Charlotte is around.

The senior pastoral ministry at your church likely falls somewhere on the spectrum between Steve and Charlotte. I would like to suggest a philosophy that I gleaned from my friend and mentor, Dr. Jeren Rowell, longtime pastor and seminary president. He suggests, "'Pastor' is an office, not an individual."

I have seen the idea of "one pastoral office with many pastors" at work, and it is a thing of beauty. The senior pastor is clearly the leader, but there is trust and homogeny in the office that allows everyone to have a role and no one to feel that their role is lesser than any other. It is the sweet spot, the circle dance, *perichoresis*—a Greek word that means "living for the other." It's healthy submission. It's cooperation. It's completion. Rowell would suggest that this sweet spot can be found when lead pastors are surrounding themselves with "who" rather than "what."

Approaching leadership positions with "what" in mind causes you to look at the position. You'll ask questions like, "What hours do I need them to be available?" and "What level of education do they have?" and "Do they have enough experience?" Asking these questions will get you to the person with the appropriate level of education, appropriate availability, and appropriate on-the-job training. It checks all the boxes. And if you lead from the *my ministry* end of the spectrum, this might work because your new leader will be able to plug and play.

Bruce Peterson suggests, "Pastoral ministry is one profession where the character of the person may be every bit as important as the skills for ministry."[1] If you're interested in moving to the *our ministry* end, you may want to look carefully at the "who." This might include questions like, "How do they get along with the rest of the staff/church leadership?" and "What are they passionate about?" and "What strengths do they bring that our leadership is currently lacking?" Asking these questions may not yield your traditional ministry leader in a particular area, but someone who will more likely fit seamlessly into the rhythms of your church's ministry.

A team can't experience *perichoresis* in the office if the members don't trust one another's abilities. One mom was actively involved in children's ministry. When her church's children's pastor left, she very much wanted to be considered to take on the role. This woman fit all of the "what" categories. She had been around children's ministry for a long time. She was educated. She was already involved. She had connections in the church. She had the availability in her schedule to do the job. On paper, she made perfect sense. The "who" categories were altogether different, however. She tended to gossip about both staff and laity. She was overly dramatic, often turning molehills into mountains. She was impetuous, rarely thinking through all of the ramifications of a decision. She would have likely been a poor addition to the leadership team at her church. Fortunately, the lead pastor recognized this and valued placing the "who" into leadership. He knew that he would not be able to trust her enough to allow her to lead. He would find himself spending extra time managing relationships she seemed to hurt and talking her down from proverbial ledges when things got tough. If you're interested in a pastoral office functioning more like a round table than a hierarchy of leadership, a senior pastor must be surrounded with trusted colleagues, not plug-and-play employees.

Finding time to spend together with your children's leader, even socially, will go a long way in establishing trust. How often is the leadership team having lunch together at your church? How often does staff meeting happen? Is there a staff retreat where all the pastors/leaders go away to think, dream, and pray together? Does the staff play together? One lead pastor I know and respect takes his staff to baseball games pretty often throughout the summer. They don't spend an extended time in prayer during these outings. They don't talk about mission or give reports. They enjoy baseball and nachos and the company of their companions in ministry. Rowell would call this collegiality and suggest that it is required to build trust within a team of leaders.

Maybe it would work in your setting to have a regular staff family dinner so the kids can all play together and spouses can join the conversation. Maybe simply having coffee with your children's leader and talking about some things other than ministry is just what you need. Just being together, with no agenda, puts coins in the relationship bank that will go a long way when the time comes that more serious matters must be addressed.

Trust is established and nurtured through extended time spent together. It is the same as the concept of working from rest, rather than resting from work. If we truly have a rhythm of Sabbath in our lives, we will be motivated to work because we're so well rested and have healthy boundaries established. Our productivity will be born out of our abundance of rest. I've seen Sabbath in staff dynamics operate the same way. If we have spent enough time simply being together, knowing one another, living life as a family group, then our functionality as a staff blossoms from that abundance of relationships built. Our trust and our ability to get on the same page (because we know each other so well) flourishes out of our time of Sabbath play and rest together.

Finally, senior pastors living nearer to the *our ministry* end of the spectrum are surrounded by fully invested leaders who have the same goals in mind. For example, let's say the staff is bringing a new children's leader into the fold and the church operates with an oft-quoted mission statement or a three-point vision. Simply reading those off to the new leader isn't enough. That's the "what." Invested leaders need the "why." Perhaps the new leader could be taken through the process that helped your church arrive at your vision. Maybe you could help your new leader articulate how the children's ministry area could live into this vision. If you're working on a new mission statement, or even something less formal that simply offers direction for your congregation, your children's leader could speak into its formation. This leader will bring a unique perspective to the table, one from which the whole staff may benefit! Work together to find what is right for your church. In this way, your children's leader is invested in the outcome and can articulate the vision from a place of passion that represents that area of ministry, instead of trying to retrofit the children's ministry to a vision into which they had little buy-in. Make it *our ministry*.

SPACE TO PASTOR

Children's leaders may sometimes be pigeonholed as event planners. The board reports I've heard, updates I've seen on social media, and countless conversations I've been in throughout the years illustrate this tendency. A typical children's leader might be in charge of a Christmas program (a musical, complete with adorable kids in animal costumes and a raffle to see who gets to play Mary this year), an Easter egg hunt, an end-of-school bash, Vacation Bible School, a back-to-school bash, and a trunk-or-treat. These productions are in addition to the smaller events like monthly preteen gatherings, district events involving other churches, church camps in the summer, lock-ins, and retreats. I don't consider myself an event-driven children's pastor by any means, but I always seem to have an event looming, demanding my attention. From my conversation with lots of children's pastors, I've even heard the lament from children's leaders that if they didn't keep all of these events going, church leadership may question the need to keep them around full time. Some of them are speculating. Others have actually heard this from their lead pastors or church boards.

I know one children's pastor who interviewed with a church leader who told her, "This is a part-time position because we're not even sure what a children's pastor would do with full-time hours." She told a group of us about this in a moment of vulnerability that can only happen among like-minded leaders who do similar jobs. After we picked our collective jaws off the floor, the other children's pastors in the circle began to list all of the things that had nothing to do with major events, and weren't directly related to Wednesdays and Sundays, that a children's ministry leader could do with full-time hours. Many of us were full time and had no problem filling fifty-plus hours each week. Mostly, it came down to a simple concept: a children's leader needs space to pastor people, not just plan events. Even if the role does not have pastor in the title (children's ministries director, for example), the pastoral nature of the role cannot be denied and requires a significant time commitment to thrive.

To illustrate my point, consider a change the children's ministry staff made at our church a few years ago. Our church had a traditional harvest party every Halloween. This included games, activities, loads of candy and other treats, inflatables, kids in costume, adults in costume—the whole enchilada. The work for this event began months in advance. To the church's credit, the entire endeavor was not put on the backs of the children's team. Adult Sunday school classes owned some of the games and food, and different volunteers who highly valued the event put in time every year. But the party was huge. The children's staff, though aided by these volunteers, would work countless hours in preparation. Thousands of dollars and significant resources were poured into the event. Then, when the night finally came, thousands of people would come through the doors, play the games, score some candy, then make their way out into the neighborhoods to do the rest of their trick-or-treating, or to other churches for similar events. In a few short hours, all of the months of preparation and thousands of dollars allocated to the night would be over. The children's team would end the evening wandering aimlessly like people emerging from a bunker in a post-apocalyptic movie. Eventually, the mess would get cleaned up and the team would be on to planning the Christmas children's musical, which was now less than two months away.

The event was considered a huge success due to the staggering number of people who walked through the door. Unfortunately, most people were so busy running the event that no one had time to make any significant connections, and most visitors were just there for the candy, one of many stops for the night. There were other churches nearby who threw similar soirées, so if a family was strategic in their planning, they could hit several churches in a five-mile radius and still get to their own neighborhood before their minivan turned back into a pumpkin.

Well-loved was the event, but our team began to question its success. Investing so much time and so many resources in one three-hour event that didn't yield significant quantifiable results and didn't directly support the church's mission and vision was suspect. The team needed space to pastor, and events like these were a significant distraction from that call.

We began thinking about a more relational, incarnational way our time and resources could be used on Halloween. While there were certainly positive things to take away from the big party, one major negative was the fact that it pulled so many of our church's people out of their homes on the one night of the year where a significant number of their neighbors would be on their doorsteps. We were missing huge opportunities to get to know our neighbors! What if we could use some of our time (though far less than planning the event) and some of our resources to help people be better neighbors and give them an opportunity to make connections and invite others to church? This would not only give our team space in the schedule to do something besides plan an event, but it would give our people space in their schedules to be pastoral in their own neighborhoods.

We concocted packets that we would give to everyone in our church. These packets would have some fun little giveaways (glow sticks, stickers, etc.) that would have our church's name and information printed on them. They would direct kids to our website, where we had a Halloween candy-themed welcome video waiting for them. We didn't spend extra money on these things, because the dollars were already allotted for the event. We included in the packets lots of ways to be extra neighborly. Turn your lights on. Give out candy along with the giveaways we've provided. Have a fire in your driveway and let trick-or-treaters roast marshmallows. Set up a hot drink station on your front porch. Take hot apple cider and cocoa out to parents who waited in cars. Make your house a must-visit house on the block.

My wife and I tried these new ideas with great success. We had people at the neighborhood pool in the summertime talking to us about our house at Halloween. I met neighbors I had never met before, even though they lived a door or two down from us. We even invited our neighbors to church, *and they showed up*. Because our church moved away from the big event, I had space to be a pastor in my neighborhood.

Months later, one of my neighbors passed away suddenly. I got the phone call asking for my help. I was a pastoral presence in the neighborhood partly because I was home to get to know people better on Halloween night. I had space to pastor.

We heard stories of other people in our church showing abundant hospitality that night. People rented popcorn machines, grilled hot dogs, set up big screens showing our welcome video on a loop. We invited people to take the efforts they would normally have put into the party and pour them into becoming a must-visit house on the block. Connections were made. Neighbors were loved.

While there was still something happening on Halloween night, it was de-centralized and incarnational in nature, rather than your traditional church event. Pastors and laity alike were given space to be a presence in their neighborhoods. Space to pastor. I tell this story to highlight what it could look like if children's leaders weren't leading one event after another. Do they have all these events because they feel pressured to? Do they know they're allowed to step back from all the planning so they have space to be pastoral in the lives of the people around them? Do they know *how* to do this, or do they need some direction from their lead pastors concerning the idea of incarnational ministry? How much time does your children's leader have to be pastoral?

Like lead pastors, children's leaders need enough margin in their lives to have space to go deep. Rather than a broad calendar, filled with traditional events, it could change the culture of your congregation to empower your children's leader with the permission to sit down with his leadership team and take a critical look at the schedule. What could drop off the list of events that allow time to actually dig deep into relationships? For example, let's say your children's ministry leader wants to invite a volunteer family over to his house for dinner as a way to get to know them better and express his appreciation. Is there enough margin in the schedule and space in the budget to make that happen?

Children's leaders need the time and the space to be pastoral in relationships with volunteers, kids and parents, neighbors on the block, other staff members, and even their own families. Your ministry leader, even if he's a volunteer with no particular call to vocational pastoral ministry, needs space to be pastoral in the lives of people around him. In this way he better represents your church and helps people feel more connected to the staff and church vision.

TITLES MATTER

One phenomenon common in children's ministry is second-career pastors. I know many children's pastors who started off as volunteers who got involved in their church's children's ministry with their own kids. My own mother, a longtime children's pastor and foundational mentor of mine, got into children's ministry with no plans to do it vocationally. She simply filled a void at church when my brother and I were little and discovered a calling that was dormant before. She went back to school, earned her master's degree, was blessed to be ordained by the church, and continues to pastor kids and families while also teaching children's ministry at the university level. She's the ultimate volunteer success story, a second-career children's pastor. I know many others whose stories follow the same basic pattern. A parent gets involved; the parent moves into a role as volunteer leader; the parent discovers a call; the parent moves into licensed, vocational ministry.

One of the ways we can show value to those with a call on their lives who have taken the initiative to become licensed or ordained ministers is to use a word of great significance with them: pastor. There is authority, education, and calling associated with the word. If your children's leader demonstrates these three things, do you acknowledge her as a pastor?

It's especially hard to move from a place of lay leadership to priestly authority within the same church. I know someone who moved slowly, over years, from volunteer leader to paid, very part-time assistant, to director, to part-time pastor, to full-time pastor. To this day, some people in the church still call him "Mr." instead of "Pastor." It took him a long time to be called "Pastor" on the bulletin. It took him longer to be called "Pastor" on the website. His transition to this vocational role lacked the intentionality of leadership helping to communicate value through title. I'm not advocating that a lay leader be called a pastor just because they're in charge. Rather, I'm advocating for those leaders who have moved officially into a licensed or ordained role and need the support of the lead pastor communicated through their title. If your children's leader is a pastor, call him "Pastor."

At the same time, concerning volunteer, non-pastoral leadership, if you're willing to give a title, be willing to make it official. Even if your children's leader is an unpaid volunteer, perhaps a dad that stepped in to fill the role, if he's willing, give him a title and put him on your staff list. Putting someone's name on the back of a bulletin and on the website list doesn't require a W-2 form. There's no IRS involvement to being given an official title. What it does, simply, is communicate value to the role. It tells the church you value children's ministry enough to name someone officially in a place of leadership. It tells your leader that his commitment matters.

A title and place in the bulletin/wherever staff is listed also gives new families a place to go with questions about children's ministry. Even in a church of fifty, there's someone visibly responsible for children's ministry. If a new family shows up on Sunday, does your staff know whom to direct them to with questions about their third grader? Do your congregants know who's in charge of children's ministry? Has it been officially communicated to your church, or have you just privately asked the highly involved dad if he would be willing to be in charge? We demonstrate value by assigning a title to the role and giving it visibility.

WHAT'S HAPPENING?

I was sitting in a staff meeting one Monday morning when our lead pastor mentioned something about his sermon the day before. Most people in the room nodded knowingly, having been sitting in the pews while he was preaching. There were a few of us, however, that had responsibilities on Sunday morning that kept us out of the "big" sanctuary. Our children's team was among those. Our lead pastor paused and said, "Oh, you guys weren't in there. Did you go back and watch my sermon online?" We hadn't, and we said as much. Realization began to dawn in his eyes. "Wait, do you guys ever go back and watch my sermons?" Sheepishly, we looked back and forth wondering who was going to be bold enough to speak up. None of us were, so we all collectively shook our heads. He realized that day that we were pretty out of the loop on what was typically happening on a Sunday morning in the sanctuary.

Most of us were filling each week with children's ministry-related tasks. We were writing lessons and sermons, planning for worship, coordinating volunteers, making videos, planning the next big event, connecting with kids and parents, coaching teams in the church's kids' sports leagues, and plenty more. Nevertheless, I completely understood where he was coming from. His sermons were the heartbeat of our congregation. He used those times, as the prophetic leader of our church, to cast vision, communicate hope for the future, tell success stories from our people, lament and respond to the brokenness in the world, and teach good, orthodox theology. The sermon is a vastly important part of what happens in the life of a congregation. Though our schedules were already full, it would have been appropriate for us to add in some listening sessions to get caught up with what most of the other adults in the church were hearing and learning on a Sunday morning.

From the seat of the children's leader, this conversation is a two-way street. My unfiltered side wanted to jump in and ask, "Are you aware of what we've been preaching in elementary worship each week? Did you know we had forty kids at the altar last Sunday laying hands on a kid who was moving away? Do you know what the thirty-plus adults that volunteer in kids' worship were hearing in children's worship?" Obviously, that would not have been an appropriate way to respond, but I might be giving you a glimpse into the inner monologue of children's pastors everywhere. It is certainly important and helpful for children's pastors to remain engaged in the adult life of the church, and vice versa.

☼ Show value by communicating that you want your children's leader connected to your preaching. Show value by communicating that you want to be connected to what your children's leader is preaching.

Certainly lead pastors have no shortage of ways to fill their time: sermon preparation, coordinating volunteers, planning events, visiting people, etc. If there is an expectation, though, for the children's leader to be in the know about what's going on in "big church," it would show great value for the lead pastor to have the same interest in children's ministry. Maybe there is a balance that can be found where both are giving a little time each month to get up to date. Not only would it show value to the children's leader for the lead pastor to be interested in what is being preached in kids' worship, but it might also be helpful as the prophetic leader of the congregation for the lead pastor to be aware of what the kids are learning and how they are engaging.

If suddenly during one staff meeting you told your children's leader that you wanted her to film her message next Sunday so you could watch it, she would likely be a nervous wreck. It would be akin to the principal unexpectedly showing up and sitting in the back of the classroom. She may feel like she had been put on the spot and had something to prove. For this reason, I don't suggest handling it this way. However, perhaps you could open up the two-way street. Tell your children's leader you would really like her to be up to date on the sermons you're preaching. It will help her connect with other adults, give them a shared story, and help her know how you're communicating the mission and vision of the church each week. But, as you suggest this, ask if there's a way she could begin filling you in on sermons she is preaching. Maybe there's already a way in place to film the children's sermons. Maybe she could film it with a smartphone and upload it somewhere for you. Maybe they could capture the audio with a free program on their presentation computer. Maybe she could give you her sermon notes, outline, or manuscript so you could see where she's headed. If she uses a curriculum, she could get you a copy of the lesson for the week. Maybe you could go sit in on children's worship one week when someone else is in the pulpit. This would connect you with a congregation in your church with whom you may not connect as often (the kids). A senior pastor closer to the *my ministry* end of the spectrum would ask that a children's leader keep up with preaching. A senior pastor near the *our ministry* end of the spectrum could ask the same thing but might create a two-way street to reciprocate the value. Show value by communicating that you want your children's leader connected to your preaching. Show value by communicating that you want to be connected to what your children's leader is preaching.

Children's leaders, like any staff members or volunteers, desire to be in the loop for the purposes of both information and relationship. Many never get an opportunity to connect with what's happening in the rest of the church. In our survey, associate staff members said:

"In my case, personally, sometimes I feel a little disconnected from the body and from the rest of the lead team because I am not often involved with regular services on Sunday."

"We serve every time we offer programs. So, there is no chance for us to really connect to others who are at the same stage of life as us."

"I feel isolated and disconnected from the rest of the church."

Finding ways to connect your children's team to the larger body brings value to your entire faith community.

GET TOGETHER

Staff meetings are a necessity. Usually, larger churches with several full-time staff members don't have a problem with this. I've had no shortage of meetings in my time in larger churches, but I've gone literally an entire year without a staff meeting as an associate in a smaller church. When everyone is part-time or volunteer, it's definitely harder to get together. When you're all in the office together every day, not only are you more likely to have a regular staff meeting, but you can also have quick hallway chats and stand-up meetings in different offices to hash out some issue or get everyone moving in the same direction on a project or idea. When your leaders don't keep regular office hours, it's still crucial that you find opportunities to be together. We talked about ways to grow in community together through play, which is important and life-giving, but finding ways to work together professionally also communicates great value. Regular meetings are a key component. Otherwise, you create parallel pastoring, where everyone is working at the same time, but never together. I have experienced this personally in a small church. I also know, from the results of our Children's Leadership Survey, that others have experienced the same things. When asked about the toughest part of leading children's ministry as a non-staff member (volunteer), the responses were things like:

"Feeling like you are out of sight, out of mind."

"Not having a voice."

"Not being able to attend staff meeting."

"They do not see value in the suggestions of a non-staff member."

"I sometimes feel like an afterthought in ministry planning."

This is especially difficult for churches that have some full-time staff and some part-time or volunteer staff. An "us and them" mentality can seep in, where the full-time staff is in the know about calendar changes, people situations, etc., around the church while the part-time or volunteer staff generally feel like they're playing catch-up. It's going to be messier, likely requiring some evening or weekend hours from time to time, but it is important to find regular opportunities to get the whole team together. This communicates value to the part-time and volunteer staff, and definitely moves you toward the *our ministry* end of the spectrum.

Board meetings are a great way to help staff feel connected as well. Especially if you have part-time or volunteer staff, this is a place for voices to be heard and value to be communicated. Value goes both ways. The children's leader feels valued at having a seat at the table and a voice that is heard. The board members see the value given to children's ministry by having this leader at the table, so your church lay leadership understands that the lead pastor values this ministry. "Some pastors allow their associates to attend board meetings?" one survey answer asked, sarcastically. "I've never attended a board meeting," answered another. Give part-time and volunteer ministry leaders opportunities to speak into the life of the church and update the rest of the leadership on what's going on in their respective areas. What are they passionate about? What do their strengths bring to the table? They will likely make a team stronger, which is why they're in that leadership role. Give them a regular place to be a part of the conversation.

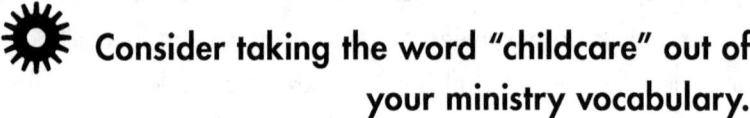 Consider taking the word "childcare" out of your ministry vocabulary.

NOT CHILDCARE

Whew. This is a biggie. Want to re-create a scene from *Braveheart*? Go to a children's ministry conference, get up on the platform, and say, "Thank you for babysitting." Oh, the carnage. This is one of the biggest hot-button issues in the world of children's ministry, and it's not unique to small churches or large churches, paid staff or volunteers.

On a Sunday off, my wife and I were looking for a local church to attend. We heard about one that was the "in" church in the area, quickly growing and making waves. I checked out their website, trying to decide if we wanted to try it out. As always, I went to the children's ministry page to see what they had to say about it. The very first thing I saw? "Childcare available starting at 9:15, ages 0-12."

Childcare available.

My wife had to talk me down. I was ready to do what any respectable internet browser would do and send a strongly worded tweet. A necessary voice of reason and perspective in my life, my long-suffering wife, reminded me there might be better ways to go about seeking change. So allow me to be a voice for the people here: consider taking the word "childcare" out of your ministry vocabulary.

Childcare, or babysitting, is what someone does while the adults do something important or special. When do you need childcare at home? Date nights. Work parties. Sure, you get someone who is fun, someone your kids like to take over for the evening, but babysitting is a placeholder. It's not about the kids. It's about the adults, and the kids need something to do in the meantime. This is an appropriate use of childcare. Please feel free to hire out as much babysitting as you like at home. But in the church, this is the opposite of communicating value. And if your children's leader is comfortable with being referred to as childcare, they may not have learned how to value the important role they fill.

Children's leaders prepare for the kids much the same way lead pastors prepare for the adults. On Sunday morning they choose appropriate music to help usher kids into a time of worship. They prepare and preach a sermon that seeks transformation in the lives of young Christians. They pray together. They play together to build community. They spend time in classrooms to disciple kids. They manage an army of volunteers who offer their free time for teaching kids and helping them feel known and loved. That's not the work of a babysitter.

Kids come to church to be known and loved. They experience a healthy model of who Jesus is through the adults with whom they come in contact. They build relationships with other Christians that will carry them through tough times and share in their joys. Their biblical literacy increases. They learn about God's love and living in it. This is not babysitting.

> ☀ **Have you ever considered that working in the nursery is in itself an act of worship? It's an investment in both the present and the future of the church.**

Yes, but what about the nursery? That's childcare, right? Spiritual formation is happening even when babies are being held. From an early age, kids are learning to feel comfortable at the church. They have multiple adults investing in their lives, telling them the same truths that their parents tell them, "You're beautiful. You are a unique creation. Jesus loves you so much." They hold babies and sing songs that teach simple truths. "Jesus loves me, this I know." Isn't that a truth we need adults to remember time and time again? We can begin to instill these truths in what we call our "youngest worshipers" in the nursery. By age one, they're able to listen to a very short story, learn the motions to a simple song, and color a picture related to what they're learning. They then play with blocks and climb on little plastic slides with their Christian brothers and sisters who will be major influencers in their lives growing up. If they stick around in the church, those kids in the nursery together will graduate together. They will spur one another toward good works in adolescence. Maybe even adulthood. They're forming Christian relationships in those simple encounters at an early age, and adults are there to guide them.

Given this lens through which to view the ministry of the nursery, can we still call it childcare?

When we refer to the nursery as childcare, not only does it devalue what's actually happening, but it sends a message to the adults who volunteer what sort of value they should give the role. If we talk about the nursery through the lens of learning, building community, etc., it challenges the adults to help that environment thrive. If we call it childcare, they will treat it that way. Challenge them to rise to the occasion.

Have you ever considered that working in the nursery is in itself an act of worship? It's an investment in both the present and the future of the church. Whether those babies have been dedicated or baptized, the congregation likely participated in some sort of liturgy committing to come alongside the parents in helping to raise their little one in the faith. Working in the nursery puts feet to that confession. When I perform baby dedications, I always look in the eyes of people in the pews and challenge them not to answer with empty words. Don't speak a liturgy back to me, or answer, "we will," if you're not really willing to invest. As an extension of this commitment, if we're truly valuing the role of the nursery worker, we're talking about the *worship* that takes place in that little, brightly colored room in the back hallway. It's an investment. It can't be children's ministry and childcare at the same time. It's one or the other.

Along the same lines, children's leaders are often the go-to people in their churches for event childcare. Allow me again to let you in on that inner monologue of a children's pastor (the things we wish we could say but never do). Children's pastors have fantasized about this conversation for years when they get together with like-minded brethren. "What if I were to call my lead pastor and be like, 'Hey, Pastor Steve, we have a preteen event coming up next Friday night. Could you please schedule something for adults to do? Our event starts at 7:00, so if you could have your adult event start at 6:45 to give the kids time to drop their parents off, then have it end at 9:30 because you know the kids like to stay and chat afterward, that would be best. I really appreciate everything you do for adultcare at our church!'" Everyone snickers, then sighs. Of course that's not a call we would make, but it's a call we've all received! If you truly buy in to the idea that children's ministry is not childcare, then calling your children's leader to schedule childcare for an event is not appropriate.

Your children's leader knows most of the people in the church who are good with kids, knows who is trained and has a background check on file, and even knows the best way to get ahold of them. So perhaps a yearly item on the staff meeting agenda can address this. Go through the annual events that typically need childcare. Have your children's leader create a list of people who might be best to call in the church to handle these events. Then, let your other leaders know that they can consult this list to get childcare for their events as they come up. I'm certain your children's leader would be thrilled to help do this pre-work, especially if it means event childcare is no longer on his plate. If this direction comes from the lead pastor, other staff members will acquiesce. If your children's leader takes it upon himself to make a childcare list, it won't be enough to get other staff members or leaders to quit contacting him for every event. He needs the lead pastor's advocacy to help the staff understand that, the same way youth ministry doesn't expect the worship arts pastor to coordinate all of their music for Wednesday nights, or the same way the worship arts pastor doesn't expect the youth pastor to manage all teenagers who sing in the choir, *children's ministry leader does not equal childcare coordinator.*

The solution can be as simple as being careful with words. Anywhere "childcare" is listed, be it on a bulletin, signage, announcement slides, or the church website, change it to "children's ministry." Anytime it is mentioned from the pulpit or during announcements, communicate the value of what children's ministry is doing through the way it is described and titled. What are kids learning at your church? How are they growing? Keep these truths in mind when talking about children's ministry, and the value will naturally flow into the description!

✺ 3 ✺
TRAINING

In my earlier days of children's ministry, I used to go to churches that had puppet ministries and train their puppeteers. You can roll your eyes at puppets if you like, but the Muppets are hilarious.

> Gonzo: Well, I want to go to Bombay, India, and become a movie star!
>
> Fozzie: You don't go to Bombay to become a movie star! You go where we're going: Hollywood!
>
> Gonzo: Sure, if you want to do it the easy way.
>
> Fozzie: We've picked up a weirdo.[1]

To this day, if a puppet shows up in the sanctuary during a Sunday morning service and starts ripping jokes on the lead pastor, everyone will be in stitches. Kids like puppets. Adults like puppets.

I would teach the budding puppeteers how to position their arms so the puppet doesn't default to staring at the sky, how to make the puppet come alive instead of just opening and closing its mouth, how to enter and exit a scene, how to develop a good voice for a character, and other tips and tricks. Puppet trainings. They're a real thing. But that's not the kind of children's ministry training we're talking about here.

I was in the middle of a master's degree when I first looked through our survey results from children's leaders. I realized that I was doing something that seemed rare in the field of children's ministry compared to other ministry areas: graduate work. Upon further digging, another rarity came to light: both my undergraduate and graduate studies are in the field of ministry and theology. Of other children's leaders in our survey, with multiple denominations represented, 26% had undergraduate degrees in theology or ministry, 22% had undergraduate degrees in education, while 25% had undergraduate degrees in various fields. This means that 47% of those surveyed had college degrees that had nothing to do with theology or ministry; 73% had an undergraduate-level education.

Considering graduate degrees, 15% of respondents reported graduate work in theology or ministry, while 14% said they had participated in graduate work in education; 6% reported graduate work in other various disciplines, meaning 20% had graduate work outside the field of theology or ministry, and the majority (65%) had no graduate work.

After looking through these results, I got curious about how lead pastors would answer similar questions. An informal survey was taken of 116 senior pastors, of varying ages and church sizes, regarding their education levels. A whopping 56% had undergraduate *and* graduate degrees in the field of theology or ministry. An additional 26% had undergraduate degrees in another field, but graduate degrees in theology or ministry. That's 82% with a graduate-level education in theology or ministry. Compare that to less than 15% of children's leaders who were educated at that level.

In our Children's Leadership Survey, children's leaders were less likely to have advanced degrees in theology or ministry than lead pastors, and were almost as likely to have a background in education as they were theology or ministry. Of those polled, 25% had undergraduate degrees in theology or ministry, compared to 23% with undergraduate degrees in education, and 27% had undergraduate degrees in entirely different fields. All told, that means twice the number of those polled had formal education in areas outside of theology and ministry. It makes sense, right? Lead pastors have to preach to adults who ask deep questions, who tend to be skeptical, and who have years of faith under their belts and need to go deeper in their learning. Children's leaders teach very young Christians who are getting to know the basics, or even younger Christians who are also learning when to alert an adult about their need to visit the bathroom in a timely manner. In other words, lead pastors have to dig into pretty complex theology, while children's leaders just have to scratch the surface. Right?

This may be the conventional thinking on the subject, but can we consider a new narrative? I heard Dr. Thomas Noble, seminary professor and former president of the Wesleyan Theological Society, speak at a conference for pastors and church leaders a few years ago. One thing in particular that stuck with me was his idea that, in order to present a simple concept, the presenter must go deep in preparation. In my own preaching, and from veteran preachers, I've learned the same sort of thing. It's hard to preach a succinct, twenty-minute sermon if you don't know the material well. Sermons that tend to be too long and too wordy can point to a preacher's lack of preparation. Someone who really knows their material inside and out can say in one sentence what someone else who only knows the material on the surface might take ten sentences to communicate. To be simple, one has to go deep.

This leads me to believe that some of our strongest theologians belong in children's ministry. If children's leaders are expected to teach foundational theological concepts to kids in our churches, and make them simple enough for their audience to understand, their training should be richly theological.

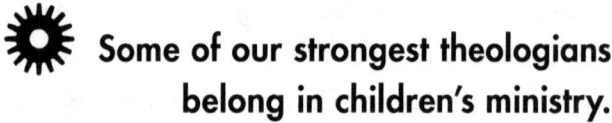

Some of our strongest theologians belong in children's ministry.

HAVE A LONG GAME

When it comes to theological training in children's ministry, it must be considered an investment in the church. Immediate returns cannot be the goal. Good training costs money. That money could be as small an investment as an e-book, or as large as a graduate degree, with lots of stops in between (classes, seminars, conferences, etc.). At whatever level, there will likely be expenses, and there may well be a member of your church board whose job it is to look at the money and ask the question, "Is this worth it?" That question can be answered, but the answer may not come for fifteen or more years.

Strong theological training, for example, does not necessarily equate to immediate church growth. That's true from any pastoral vantage point. Just because a pastor has a solid grasp on the church's theological tradition does not mean people will come in droves to hear truth preached—nevertheless, we would all agree on that theological training's importance. In the building blocks of pastoral ministry, great theology is foundational. It informs all else.

Sound theological training for children's leaders, then, isn't immediately about church growth. It is, however, foundational to a strong children's ministry. Sound theology prevents un-teaching, or re-teaching in adulthood. If children's leaders know not only what to teach but how to teach it, the ground work is laid for youth and then young adults to build on a great foundation. This means their future pastors don't have to spend a lot of time re-teaching basic theological concepts in adulthood and instead can focus on growing mature disciples. Mature disciples can be expected to go and make disciples. This is church growth. Though the rewards might be in the future, the investment is happening now. We can expect a return on our investment in theological training. Some of it will be right away. Some will be in the years to come.

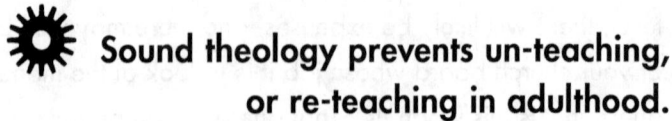 **Sound theology prevents un-teaching, or re-teaching in adulthood.**

RESIDENT TRAINER

Let's start with the lead pastor. As the resident theologian and staff leader, the lead pastor has the best platform to offer theological training to the rest of the staff. In my first full-time pastoral assignment, I was hired alongside a first-time youth pastor. We were wide-eyed newbies with the whole pastoral world in front of us. Our lead pastor was keenly aware of just how green we were and excellent at orientation, always thinking through the details from a "what do the new kids need to know?" point of view. He invested wisdom in us concerning hospital visitations, pastoral counseling, dressing like professionals (that one time I wore flip flops on a Sunday morning, I'll never forget the look I received that only mothers and senior pastors can give), and so much more. I'll always remember some of the truths he instilled in me. One of the greatest, though, was perhaps unintentional.

Each week, our lead pastor would sit down with the pastors and spend the first half of staff meeting bouncing ideas around about upcoming sermons. Sometimes he would talk at length about the train of thought, scripture, or tradition that had brought him to a particular nugget of truth over which he was mulling. Sometimes he would ask a question and spend much of the rest of the meeting listening. I rarely spoke up in my first six months. Looking at the spiritual giants to my right and left, I felt woefully underqualified to add to the discussion. I vividly remember the first time I decided I had something worth voicing. I actually raised my hand, which no one ever did. After a good-natured ribbing at my diplomacy, they let me speak. I began with, "I realize I don't have the training or experience that all of you have, but I was thinking—" and he cut me off. He told me that he wanted to hear what I had to say, but he needed to make it very clear that he never wanted to hear me offer that qualifier again. He said he recognized pastoral gifts and graces in me, which was why I was sitting at the table. Sitting at the table was permission enough to engage. I finished my thought, feeling empowered.

Those discussions took me to the deep end of the theology pool. I wanted to add to them, and occasionally did after being empowered to do so, but more than that I wanted to remember everything I was hearing. I took lots of notes, like I was in a classroom. As my qualifying statement denoted, I didn't have the experience or the training that my lead pastor or others in the room had. Their discussion was a gift. It didn't cost them any extra dollars in training, but it gave me lots of opportunities to grow.

Lead pastors likely have a significant library from their time in ministry and formal training. Sharing formational books with a staff pastor, even reading a book together as a staff, is a low-cost way of training. If we've all read the same book, we will have shared language and a shared approach to a particular subject. If a lead pastor is hoping to inspire a staff to think the way she does, inviting them all to read something together that articulates this way of thinking will be a great way to invite communal thinking and shared ethos.

In general, if all leaders can simultaneously see themselves as teachers and learners, a balance can be struck with the staff. As experts in their respective areas, each staff member likely has much to teach the rest of the staff. Each can also learn from the others. What if the lead pastor sought out opportunities to teach, using that theological training to better prepare the other pastors on staff? I learned a lot from my first lead pastor, including how to situate myself to genuinely listen to the expertise coming from the rest of the staff. Together, we were better.

OTHER TRAINING NEEDED

In our survey of children's leaders, we asked where people felt they lacked training. Of the options given, some were more children's ministry specific, like lesson writing, classroom management, and child development. Others were broader pastoral concepts, like leadership, theology, preaching, and pastoral care and counseling. What we learned was that children's leaders feel much more equipped in the areas related specifically to children's ministry. The top answers were the latter four above, with pastoral care and counseling being the runaway favorite for training needed.

As a children's pastor, pastoral care and counseling has always been a subject I need to study more. It was also the subject I studied the least since it wasn't where my skill set was the strongest. We like to study what we enjoy and what we're good at. As I realized that I was weak in the area of pastoral care, I began forcing myself to read and study. I went to seminars and bought books (some of which still remain unread) on the subject of pastoral counseling in hopes of becoming an expert.

Apparently I don't stand alone in my feelings of inadequacy. Of those polled in our Children's Leadership Survey, 50% said they lacked training in this area. It can be overwhelming. In children's ministry we have to deal with many of the same things lead pastors deal with, but from the child's point of view. We all know significant times in children's lives can impact them far into their adult years, so children's leaders are treading lightly. We don't want to mess this up! While a lead or counseling pastor might be dealing with divorce, the children's leader is facing the child impacted by that divorce, confused and vulnerable like their parents. Children's leaders are counseling kids dealing with bullies, absent parents (single-parent households), puberty, home finances (kids overhear and internalize these conversations), grief and loss, sibling struggles, the introduction of pornography, moving, unwelcome change that upsets their security, and plenty more. Often, they are victims of these situations because they don't have much say in them. Kids can't control how much money their parents have, whether they have to move for their dad's new job, or what websites their older teenage brothers are leaving open on the family computer. Counseling adults can often be traced back to choices they made. Counseling kids can also often be traced back to the choices adults made. This puts children's leaders who are playing a counseling role in kids' lives in a precarious position that must be handled with great care. Oftentimes, the conversations they'll have won't come in a formal counseling session. Instead, a vulnerable child will speak about something going on at home in the hallways at church as quickly as she speaks about how her day at school was. It can come across as flippant, but the response from the adult has to be anything but flippant. Children's leaders need training on these micro-counseling sessions, as well as dealing with more official opportunities when kids and parents need a more focused audience.

Leadership was another major area where the surveyed children's leaders felt they lacked training. This is cause for concern, because children's leaders likely lead the largest group of volunteers in any given church (which we'll talk more about in the next chapter). A children's leader must be a competent leader not only of kids but also of adults. This includes conducting meetings, managing schedules, casting vision, articulating and perpetuating a philosophy of ministry, dealing with lots of personality types in teaching/leadership roles, mentoring younger volunteers, etc. Children's ministry often involves several students from the youth group working as volunteers as well. This means children's leaders are expected to be capable leaders of human beings newborn through the oldest volunteer (who may be in her eighties). This includes several very distinct personality types. All of this must fall in the children's leader's repertoire. Leadership training is of the utmost importance. The army of volunteers (spanning about sixty years of age) needs a general. The kids in the church also need a pastoral guide, which points to another area of training where children's leaders say they need help: preaching.

Whether your children's leader is on a large platform in front of three hundred kids with lights, a full band, and an intricate set design, or he's in front of twelve elementary students somewhere in the basement with nothing but a Bible and a felt board, he is preaching. Using the word "preaching" is another way to speak value into the role, but it is not a misnomer. A children's leader investing in kids with sound biblical teaching, pursuing a goal of transformation in their lives, is a preacher. Not every children's leader feels a call to preach. A children's leader may simply be reading verbatim from the page in a curriculum. Either way, as a church leadership team, take the opportunity to raise the bar and demonstrate value by calling preaching exactly what it is.

☀ Permission to preach needs to be given to children's leaders so they have the confidence to call a sermon a sermon. Then, they need further training on preparing and delivering that sermon.

I can't count on my fingers and toes how many times I've said something like, "I was actually preaching about that last Sunday" or "In my sermon prep last week . . ." and I'm met with, "Oh, you preached last week?" I always respond saying I indeed preached in children's worship. This usually gets something like, "Oh, right. I thought you meant you *preached* preached." I know what this means, and I know it is said innocently, but perhaps our language could change. Children's leaders can preach every week to kids like lead pastors do to adults. You may hear children's leaders say something like, "I'm more of a teacher anyway," or, "I don't preach, I just tell stories." Permission to preach needs to be given to children's leaders so they have the confidence to call a sermon a sermon. Then, they need further training on preparing and delivering that sermon.

Training in the art and discipline of preaching is widely available. This includes at least theology, leadership, hermeneutics, ecclesiology, exegesis, and public speaking. Preaching to kids also incorporates studies into learning styles (though I would add that engaging in multi-sensory preaching for adults is also a great idea), and child development. Becoming a better preacher is no easy task, but it ranks near the top of areas in which children's leaders crave further training.

INVESTMENT IN PARENT TRAINING

Finally, an important component of training includes parents. If kids were in church every single Wednesday and Sunday, which describes very few, children's leaders would have access to them three hours a week. That's at the top end, in a perfect world, but we'll use three hours for argument's sake. Let's look at a typical week for a kid:

    168 hours

    -40 for school (including bus rides)

    -70 for sleeping (ideally)

    -10 for extracurriculars (piano, baseball, gymnastics)

-3 for church (in our utopian model)

=45 hours.

That's forty-five hours, give or take, a parent has left to schedule for their kids. Even if some of that is spent with a babysitter to account for extra parent work hours, we're still talking about parents having ten times the hours to invest in their kids as the church's measly 180 minutes. This doesn't even take into account the influence parents have over their kids. Their words carry weight. While we have a voice, parents are their kids' heroes and primary influencers. Parents define much of what kids believe about the world. If a parent's Christian worldview is somehow skewed, or if it doesn't exist, their children will likely need a lot of teaching, un-teaching, and re-teaching as youth and young adults.

Children's leaders can help parents realize the significance of their own role in their children's lives. Parents can benefit from training on teachable moments, family Bible studies, discerning entertainment options for their kids, internet safety, appropriate conversations to have within earshot of kids, choosing mentors for their kids outside the family, and so much more. Parent training is crucial to the health of a children's ministry and the life of a church in the long view.

Here are a few ideas for training parents in the church.

1. Parenting seminars. Once a quarter, host a parenting seminar at a time when you know your people respond. Perhaps it's during your regular Sunday school hour or on a Wednesday night. Don't let it go unnoticed. Teach about the value of the seminar from

the platform. Talk about the influence parents have on their kids' lives. Either use pastors to lead these or bring in local "experts" for added pull and knowledge. These might even present opportunities to partner with other churches in your immediate area.

2. Parent library. Invest in a few books that cover several key areas in parenting. If possible, include recommendations from your pastoral staff. These can be short write-ups with brief synopses and reasons to pick up each book. Perhaps place these recommendations sticking out of the book on a laminated sheet or in signage nearby. Endorsements from trusted leaders go a long way in getting people to read something new. Put all the books in a certain, properly labeled area and allow them to be borrowed or checked out. Make sure pastors and leaders know what's in the library so they can direct parents to certain titles in conversations and counseling sessions.

3. Include parent training in regular communication. Do you have a weekly e-newsletter or a frequent presence on social media? Use the wealth of knowledge online to continue offering resources to parents. There are many high-quality blogs and videos meant to teach and inspire.

WHERE ELSE TO GET TRAINING

We've covered some potential children's ministry training platforms that don't cost much. I would suggest these be standard and ongoing in the church. Further training to offer life and depth into this ministry is available as well. Remember, putting budget dollars into children's ministry isn't always about immediate returns. It's an investment into young Christians right now, and it's an investment into the sort of adults and church leaders the kids in your church will become.

Conferences offer a wealth and breadth of knowledge that likely represent what your church's children's leader needs and desires. These require a financial investment, so they may not work for every church size. Or, it may take significant pre-planning to make them happen if your church decides (maybe after reading this book) that the value is high enough! I won't list all of the children and family leadership conferences that are out there, as the landscape is likely to change as this writing endures. There are four general children's ministry conference types of which ministry leaders should be aware:

1. Broad focus. These conferences tend to offer the gamut of training a children's leader might need: pastoral care and counseling, preaching, teaching, classroom management, storytelling, volunteers, you name it. These conferences seem broad, but because of the wealth of knowledge within, strategic children's leaders can set customized tracks that fit exactly what they need.

2. Family ministry. These conferences tend to look at all aspects of ministry through an intergenerational lens, searching for ways to bring the church together across age lines. Often, these are not just for children's leaders, but church leadership in general.

3. Spirituality. These children's ministry conferences delve further into theology and spiritual formation in children. The range of

focus doesn't represent the broad reach of the standard children's ministry gatherings, but are much more intent on certain areas, like spiritual development, biblical models for family ministry, or even expounding upon scholarly papers. These conferences might appeal to the more seasoned children's leader who is looking for depth.

4. Publishing. There are conferences run by certain publishers that tend to give more attention to curriculum and products produced by that publisher. Most of them are careful not to make the conference a commercial, but are best attended by churches already using or very interested in using that publisher's materials. Many of them will offer trainings specific to their curricula, or have their books' authors leading workshops. If your church has bought into a specific curriculum or if you have a brand you really trust, this sort of conference might be beneficial.

Conferences are also good for Sabbath, as children's leaders get away from normal life for a few days. Often there is opportunity to go with other children's leaders or friends in similar ministry situations. The nature of the getaway is something that children's leaders don't often get. Every year at the children's leadership conference with which I am involved, I hear people say, "I never get to be a part of worship! I always have a job to do!" These conferences offer an opportunity to be Mary, when so much of ministry feels more like Martha. They can be life-giving events. Children's leaders come home renewed, ready to work from their rest, rather than rest from their work!

Beyond conferences, there are several places online for children's leaders to complete certifications in children's ministry. These certifications can be likened to a deeper version of what one might experience attending a broad children's ministry conference. They would include volunteer recruitment, leadership, preaching and teaching, and more. If your church has a children's leader with no formal training, this certification might give parents confidence that their kids are in good, educated hands without your children's leader having to receive a degree in children's ministry.

As a first step in moving forward with a training initiative, your leadership team could sit down with the children's leaders and talk about some training goals. What are the children's ministry team's hopes for the future? Where is training lacking? Where does the children's leader need confidence? What has been the feedback from parents? How effective is the current curriculum? Where can children's ministry be better? From this conversation, the proper training outlet may emerge.

When possible, it would be helpful to build some training money into the children's leader's budget or employment package. I've seen this structured two ways: (a) There is a line item in the children's ministry budget for conferences, which might only include enough for the leader to go, or might include enough for the leader and a key volunteer or two to attend; (b) There is an addition to a hired leader's salary package that is for education, whatever that may look like. This could include books purchased, conferences attended, or classes taken. The use of those monies would be at the children's leader's discretion. This could also include education that is not specifically related to children's ministry, but may benefit the role. Perhaps filmmaking classes would bolster the ministry if more video is being considered. Perhaps graphic design classes could step up the aesthetics of children's ministry materials. An education fund of whatever size offers the children's leader freedom to do some ministry assessment and introspection to find an opportunity that meets the needs discovered. As always, this assessment should be done along with the lead pastor so agreement is reached on what area needs the most focus.

✺ 4 ✺
VOLUNTEERS

Eighty-seven. That's how many people were volunteering in children's ministry in my first assignment. I took over the role from a strong team-builder with volunteer health at an all-time high. The eighty-seven volunteers included nursery, early childhood, and elementary, Sunday school, children's worship, and mid-week programming. To be counted on this list, they had to serve regularly, on a monthly or weekly rotation. This was a mid-sized church. Eighty-seven represented roughly a quarter of the congregation. It did not include the all-hands-on-deck events like VBS, where many extra volunteers were recruited for a weeklong intensive. This army of eighty-seven volunteers was investing in kids on a weekly or monthly basis. What a gift!

I'd love to tell stories about how this volunteer core thrived under my leadership. But with little training on how to manage, love, recruit, or train volunteers, the number slowly waned during my tenure. While other aspects of the ministry were successful, I lacked a significant understanding about maintaining volunteer health. I rode the coattails of the strong teams already built, and watched it methodically erode over the years without the tools to bring it back together.

When I was called to my next assignment, I recognized my need for growth. I wanted volunteers to be a priority because they are key to the health of children's ministry. In my next role, we brought some key people onto our staff to focus specifically on volunteer health, and our team of children's pastors put our heads together to create both a system of recruiting and management, and a strategic approach to continued volunteer wellness. In sharing what we learned, I want to be careful to acknowledge that team. Our children's ministry staff was strongest when we all worked together, and what I learned about a healthy culture of volunteerism came from this whole group.

It's also worth noting here that eighty-seven may seem like a ridiculously huge number for pastors of smaller churches. It may seem unattainable. Let me encourage you to read this chapter through a lens of your own church's size. My eighty-seven may be your five or fifteen. Don't get caught up in your number of volunteers. The systems laid out in this chapter can be applied at any church large enough to have a children's leader (paid or volunteer).

ARMY OF EIGHTY-SEVEN

Can you think of any recruited group in your church that represents 25% of your congregation? That's a huge number! When volunteerism is at its healthiest in children's ministry, it will likely be the largest recruited team in your church. Due to safety policies, ratios, crowd control, and the value of mentorship, children's ministry tends to employ lots of volunteers. In addition to all the teachers, split up by age levels, there are people to keep up resource rooms, hallway monitors, greeters, and check-in managers. There is often some sort of worship service that will include a pastor or volunteer teacher, a worship leader, mentors, puppeteers, and a sound technician. Mid-week programming will employ many of the same positions seen during Sunday morning discipleship hours. Lots of these volunteers work on a rotation basis, teaching weekly or monthly, so many positions require double the number of people it actually takes to fill the role. When you consider filling all those positions, birth through preteens, with many on monthly rotations, needing eighty-seven volunteers in a mid-sized church doesn't seem like such a huge number. But actually enlisting eighty-seven volunteers . . . that's like recruiting an army. A daunting task. Maintaining your volunteer force is an even more daunting task. Putting a system in place that can be trusted is key.

GAINING INTEREST

Before we strategize about how to get people plugged in, we should look at who we're after and how we're going to get them to take the first step. Building interest in children's ministry is done primarily in two ways: duty and calling. The first one may seem easier, but the second one yields the sort of results you're likely after.

Duty speaks primarily to parents of kids. The overall philosophy of this recruiting method says, "You've got a kid in children's ministry, so you need to get involved." Some parents automatically want to be involved because they desire to be a part of their kids' spiritual formation, or because they really want to know their kids' friends, or because work keeps them away from their kids so they want to use church as a time to further connect, or because they're genuinely looking for a place to plug in. If a parent wants to get involved, jump on it! But calling upon a parent's "duty" to volunteer in children's ministries, essentially asking them to pay their dues for having children in the first place, might not yield the strongest volunteer core.

 **Familiar faces build trust.**

Appealing to a person's perception of God's call, on the other hand, says, "We're looking for people who care about ministry to children. If God is calling you to get involved, we want you!" This group may include parents, but it can also include overlooked groups in the church like retirees, empty nesters, young singles, and child-free couples.

I've worked with volunteers from both sides of the duty/calling coin. I've seen amazing things from each group. From the calling group, though, I have seen the most in-depth engagement and longevity.

Consider my friend Kelly who began volunteering in ministry to preteens well over a decade ago. She's a thirty-something single professional who volunteers in children's ministry because she feels called to do so. She has been a mainstay in the preteen Sunday school classroom and at all their events for so long she's now attending old preteens' weddings and watching them bring babies to the nursery.

I can tell stories of others like Kelly. Because she wasn't volunteering out of duty, she didn't move up from class to class as her children grew and she didn't leave children's ministries when her kids entered the youth group. I recognize that parents who follow this pattern often make up a majority of the volunteer core and should be greatly appreciated, but the more volunteers who come out of calling, the more steadfast your ministry will become. This will also build trust with parents who have multiple kids. Each year they will come back with their kids one year older and they will always see your version of Kelly greeting at her Sunday school door. They will gain confidence that children's ministry is strong and a great place to be because volunteers stick around. Familiar faces build trust.

Recruiting from a person's call requires extra effort. It involves storytelling and philosophy. It involves vision casting. This sort of recruiting cannot be done through an announcement scrolling on the screen pre-service, or a blurb in the bulletin about the need for teachers.

Here's an example:

I invited Brad up onto the platform during service. Brad was a young adult and had grown up in the church. I told a little bit of Brad's story. "Many of you know Brad because you've seen him grow up in this church. You saw him go to preschool here. You saw him in the youth group. Now you see him greeting at the south door every Sunday. Brad also volunteers as an assistant teacher in junior high Sunday school each week. He not only grew up here. When he left home, he decided to stay here. Can you talk to me about why you stuck around, Brad?"

Brad answered confidently. "I did grow up in this church and many people poured their time, love, knowledge, and energy into me. I am who I am today because of my parents and the people in this church. I want to do the same thing for kids here today, so they can tell a similar story in a few years, and I can be a part of it."

Brad and I had talked beforehand and gone over what he was going to say. I didn't give him the words, but I let him throw all of his words out there and suggested which ones he could best use to tell a succinct version of his story. It wasn't contrived. He wasn't a professional public speaker. He was a guy who had been shaped by the church and in turn was doing what he'd been taught to do by all of those adults in his life.

Brad's story showed people hope for the future. It was a success story and pointed people to very simple ways that they could be a part of more stories like his. Brad had a calling to shape the youth of the church because he had been so significantly shaped by volunteers who loved him as a kid. How many people in your church today were shaped by volunteers who loved them as a kid? It's probably a large number—help them remember their own stories and show them how they can be a part of a new one. This is recruiting through helping parishioners discover their calling.

THE LEAD PASTOR

The lead pastor is an important voice in guiding people to explore the ways in which God is calling them to serve. Word from the pastor carries significant weight in the congregation. Something that could be easily overlooked as just another announcement in a long line of announcements, including an upcoming prayer meeting, a youth retreat, and sign-ups in the foyer for this or that, becomes significant when it stands on its own and is highlighted by the prophetic leader of the congregation.

In our Children's Leadership Survey, we asked how church leadership helps in recruiting volunteers. Many children's leaders' answers started with "they don't." There was some obvious frustration in the overwhelming task of recruiting volunteers and the general lack of support being felt by those surveyed. Some answered that support came through space given to children's ministry to recruit. For example, one answer said, "They allow us to show videos in the service and we can put stuff in the worship folder and set up tables in the foyers to recruit." There were many that expressed a similar situation. They are allowed space to do their recruiting, but they aren't receiving help in the actual process.

Imagine if the senior pastor was the one to call Brad up and help tell his story. Then, the sermon pointed people toward serving in the faith community. Imagine a sermon, or even a series, that inspired hearers to get involved and pointed people directly toward opportunities to which they may feel called. The sermon would be immediately applicable!

Lead pastors have a natural platform with adults in the church that children's leaders don't have. If a children's leader wants to get something out in front of parents and other adults, they often go through a rigorous process of creating newsletters, jockeying for space in some other printed communication piece, asking for permission to make an announcement on Sunday morning, or seeking people out one by one. The lead pastor has the attention of the majority of the church's adults every single Sunday. Church-wide awareness of the value of children's ministry can be raised significantly through the consistent verbal support of the senior pastor.

> **Church-wide awareness of the value of children's ministry can be raised significantly through the consistent verbal support of the senior pastor.**

Preaching sermons isn't the only way a lead pastor can get involved. Finding ways to actually volunteer in children's ministry also speaks volumes. I know a pastor who preaches in children's worship on a regular basis (several times a year). That may seem extreme to you, but there is no doubt that children's ministry is highly valued in that church. People notice. People act. The lead pastor's words *and* actions carry significance. Buy-in from that position goes a long way in communicating value and inspiring people to act when it comes to volunteering in children's ministry!

A RECRUITING SYSTEM

So, we know who we're after (people who will serve because they feel called to do so). A simple system can smooth out the process. Creating a system builds trust with volunteers, builds trust with parents, and creates a perpetual recruiting window through which interested pre-volunteers can get more info and find a place to plug in. Let's look at some of the basic building blocks.

First, in a productive volunteer recruiting system, there is always a place for new volunteers to get started. Never miss an opportunity! If someone is new to the church and they want to talk about children's ministry, if someone hears a story and wants to get involved, or something has piqued a person's interest, where are they going to go? We can capture those opportunities by establishing an information station, or with a blurb in the bulletin that clearly identifies whom to contact about serving with children. The greeters, ushers, or other first-impression team members should all know the answer to this question. They should also be coached to alert the children's leader so a personal contact can be made as soon as possible. Strike while the iron is hot!

When someone on the children's team follows up with a personal contact, it is important to have next steps in place so the recruiting moves forward. Don't call just to say, "It's so great that you're interested! Yeah, let me look and see what's going on. I'm sure we've got something for you!" Rather, answer confidently. "We would love to have you in children's ministry! Our next volunteer meeting is two weeks from tonight, in the fellowship hall, at 7:00 p.m. Can you come to that so we can talk about the next step in joining the team?" There is a place for pretty much every skill set in children's ministry! For our church's system, this next step was a meeting every other month during the Sunday school hour. We would advertise for two weeks leading up to the meeting. The broad advertisements would say something like, "If you're interested in getting involved in children's ministry, or if you have questions about it, come!" We would also extend personal invitations to those who had shown any sign of interest in the weeks leading up to the meeting. This informational session became part of the church's normal rhythm. Its regularity gave leadership something to point to for step one of ministry involvement. Sometimes no one came. We would set out the donuts and the signage and do all the advertising and sit in an empty room for forty-five minutes. Sometimes two or three people showed up. Sometimes we were surprised by the larger-than-normal response. No matter what, though, we kept it on the calendar. That's key to any good system. Stay true to it even when no one is currently moving through it. When the time comes, the system is active and ready to help. Keeping it on the calendar also proved helpful because people would show up that none of us knew had any interest in children's ministry. They could fall through the cracks of personal contact from someone on our team, but they were directed to the class by a greeter or another pastor because the class was consistent. There was always a place to send people.

Once in the class, interested persons got an overview of children's ministry, they met a staff member or two, they were given necessary volunteer paperwork (no one left the room without a volunteer packet), and they discussed where they could see themselves thriving in ministry. Occasionally, people will come through the system that don't fit into a traditional role. Not everyone that came through was a master teacher. There's always room for greeters, singers, or resource room organizers! Or, on the flip side, you may not currently have the numbers to staff so many different positions. This would mean that your teacher's job description may be more robust. They may serve as teacher, greeter, and resource room organizer. With an effective recruitment system your ministry will begin to gain more volunteers, allowing you to relieve your teachers of some responsibilities so they can focus on teaching. As you make these transitions, help people who are managing multiple roles (e.g., teaching/greeting/organizing/check-in) determine which one of those roles would be best to hand off to a new volunteer.

☀ It's okay if people say no, but they can't say yes if you don't ask.

Some volunteers started at a very entry-level, low-stress volunteer role and slowly moved to a role with more responsibility as they felt comfortable. It's important to have these entry-level positions available, so know them ahead of time.

Coming out of the class, we always followed up with each attendee, even if they said they weren't interested during class. We wanted to thank them for attending and listening. We wanted to give them another opportunity to say yes, or even force them to say no again. It's okay if people say no, but they can't say yes if you don't ask.

This recruiting system was always at work. If someone was interested in volunteering following our meeting, we would get their paperwork (application, references, background check), meet with them for a volunteer interview, walk them through safety and policy training (more on that later), and get them placed in their new position! This would usually take a couple of weeks. Sometimes there were three or four people moving through the system all at once. Sometimes there was no one. But the system was always ready for new recruits.

The system built trust with both volunteers and parents. Volunteers knew we valued the position enough to be recruiting and to have several steps in place that reiterated safety and training. We didn't just meet someone in the foyer and stick them in a classroom the next week. By choosing to walk through the process, we knew they were likely committed enough to stick around. When it's as easy as a two-minute conversation to get into a leadership role in ministry, it's also easy to get out. When there are steps to get in and someone is willing to take each of those, it raises the commitment level. At first, we were afraid volunteers would balk at having to jump through hoops to be involved, but instead we received appreciative feedback because the roles felt valuable.

The system built trust with parents because they recognized how much effort the team was putting into placing quality volunteers in places they would thrive. A parent knew that every teacher, greeter, helper, or mentor had been through the same training, filled out the same paperwork, and had been vetted and placed by a member of the children's staff.

This sort of system can work in any size church. Instead of having fifteen to twenty new volunteers move through the system each year, a smaller church might only see one or two. I know lots of smaller churches, though, that would love to move one or two new people into children's ministry with regularity each year, especially if those people stick around. The process isn't about recruiting loads of new volunteers at once. Rather, it's about systematically building a core of called volunteer ministers who endure, while other volunteers, involved more out of duty than calling, move in and out of children's ministry.

LOVING VOLUNTEERS

Thinking systematically shouldn't end with recruiting. Helping volunteers continue to feel appreciated and equipped is important to their long-term health and endurance. It is wise to employ at least two yearly appreciation methods and two equipping methods. One of each of these should be very regular, perhaps monthly. The other can be something done quarterly or biannually.

Appreciating volunteers can be as simple as note writing. Make it a point to write a handwritten note to at least two volunteers every week. It can either be general or related to something specific you recently saw or heard about. Find a weekly rhythm for note writing. The lead pastor could even help write a specified number of notes each month. If you have eighty-seven volunteers, that's less than four short notes per week and every volunteer will have received two notes in a year. It's a discipline, to be sure. Call me old-fashioned, but a hand-written note still goes a long way.

A couple of times a year, you could do something extra special for volunteers that helps them know they're loved. Invite the whole team over to your house for a baked potato bar. If the team is too big, invite them in groups broken up by when they serve (Sunday school, Wednesday night, etc.) or whom they serve (pre-k, early elementary, etc.). If you aren't comfortable hosting at your house, host it at another staff member's house, or even at the church. Evenings hard to do? Surprise everyone with biscuits and gravy or a breakfast casserole on a Sunday morning. Are you getting the theme? Give volunteers food!

Another perpetual appreciation method is a volunteer hangout space that is available whenever there is children's ministry programming taking place. Provide donuts, coffee, granola bars, and a place for volunteers to get to know each other and take a deep breath before the storm (of kids) hits. This can be its own room or simply a corner of the hallway. Help volunteers know they have a space that is specifically set apart because you have them in mind.

Continual equipping is also important. I would suggest at least two volunteer trainings a year. Each can focus on something different. Perhaps the fall training can be on classroom management while the spring training can focus on building relationships with kids. Perhaps one training can be practical while another is mostly philosophical. Choose topics that work for your context. Help volunteers share your vision, language, and tools for success in the classroom.

For consistent equipping, slipping short blurbs into curriculum folders for teachers or on rotating signage in your volunteer space is a great way to offer quick tips and inspiration. A regular volunteer communication piece (e-newsletter, Facebook group, etc.) that offers reminders of philosophy and simple, practical suggestions works wonders. Always be looking for ways to help volunteers feel equipped to do their jobs with excellence.

AFTER HOURS HOURS

Working with an army of eighty-seven is no small task. Some of the volunteers are students. Some are young professionals. Some are stay-at-home moms. Some are retirees. Connecting with them personally and corporately requires quite a bit of finagling, and quite a few nights and weekends. Children's leaders need permission to keep some irregular office hours in order to keep up with the tall task of volunteer connections.

My wife and I have always had volunteers over to our house for dinner. We slowly work through the volunteer Rolodex, hoping to make connections with as many as possible. I have been fortunate enough to be allowed flexible hours for this sort of ministry, but many children's leaders face more rigid expectations. I know staff pastors who have to log a certain number of in-office hours every week. I know staff pastors who are required to get permission for any ministry that is happening during office hours that pulls them away from the church campus. Some children's leaders are volunteers and aren't expected to keep regular office hours. I recognize that the spectrum from flexibility to rigidity is wide. It's important to consider, with a large volunteer core, the number of hours that might need to be spent connecting in the evenings and on weekends.

If a children's leader is having dinner or coffee with volunteers, hosting trainings, or developing leadership teams in the evenings because that's when the majority of volunteers are available, it is helpful if they have the flexibility to be away from the office some during the day. Since their evenings are full of ministry, some daytime hours need to be used to connect with their own families or take some time off. It's helpful when a lead pastor can recognize how much work goes into volunteer connections outside of normal office time and can offer adaptable office hours to compensate.

✻ 5 ✻
INTERGENERATIONAL MINISTRY

For me, intergenerational ministry starts with volleyball in my backyard growing up. My parents would string a net from our basketball goal across the backyard to our playhouse. (The playhouse was built on stilts. We wanted a treehouse, but we didn't have a tree in the backyard, so Dad compromised and built us a playhouse in the air.) And everyone, adults and kids alike, still full from all the hamburgers and deviled eggs that had just been consumed, would play volleyball in the backyard until it was too dark to see.

Let me back up. I grew up in a small Midwestern town in a small Midwestern church. We had church Sunday morning, Sunday night, and Wednesday night. The church was everything in my family. It was our social life, our way of serving, our way of developing our gifts (I learned to sing, act, and write in the church), and so much more. It was down the street from our house, so it's where my brother and I played roller hockey in the parking lot, where we established a clubhouse in the garage attic, and where we built snow forts in the winter. Other than my nuclear family, the church was the most central player in my childhood.

It was not at all uncommon in the summertime for my mom to ask the pastor to announce after Sunday evening service, "The Tylers have graciously opened their home to anyone who would like to come over tonight. Grab a snack to share and meet in their backyard!" While my wife and I love to host people in our home now, I've never offered an invitation to the entire church at once! My parents were hospitality rock stars. My dad would rush straight home and fire up the grill, and within a half hour people would begin to show up, changed into comfortable clothes, with bags of chips, plates of brownies, trays of deviled eggs, and whole watermelons. We'd lay it all out on a picnic table in the backyard, string up the volleyball net, and we'd hang out until people decided it was bedtime.

Those are memories that would certainly stick with me for nostalgia's sake alone, but little did I realize that they were significantly shaping my philosophy of ministry.

"Intergenerational" wasn't a buzzword then. It seems every church now is either striving to be intergenerational, or they're admitting to not being very intergenerational with a rather helpless, guilty look on their faces. It feels overwhelming, and many aren't sure where to start. In our survey to children's leaders, we didn't ask specifically whether their churches were doing intergenerational ministry, but rather about their definition of it and how it lines up with their lead pastor's definition. There were many responses that said something like, "Not sure" or "I don't know what his thoughts are" or "This hasn't been discussed." We'll talk more about getting on the same page, but clearly many leaders haven't even opened the book. One response was very succinct: "We don't do intergenerational ministry."

Are you sure?

DEFINE IT

A children's pastor I know was hired at a large church. He was educated and had years of experience in professional children's ministry when he first sat down with the lead pastor. The lead pastor was also fairly new at this church and had lots of ideas about how he wanted to see ministry happen. "I want this church to be known for being a family church, an intergenerational church," said the lead pastor to the new children's pastor. "If there was one thing I would want to be remembered for, it would be intergenerational ministry."

"That sounds great!" The new children's pastor was very excited at this prospect. Ministering to whole families was near and dear to his heart. It sounded like this lead pastor was swinging the door wide open to invest into family ministry at the church. The two left the meeting excited about the future.

While many amazing things happened in that future that is now the past, one thing became quite clear: the lead pastor and the children's pastor had very different ideas of what intergenerational ministry was. The lead pastor saw it as an event-driven ministry, where extra things might be added to the calendar, or tacked on to existing ministries, that would include families. He also saw it as adding kid-related programs onto existing programs, like adding a "children's element" to a Christmas Eve service. The children's pastor saw intergenerational ministry as a re-imagining of present ministries, finding ways to engage all ages in what already existed. This might look like changing the very way the Christmas Eve service is done to include or engage kids in the different service elements, rather than adding an extra element that is just for kids. The children's pastor also saw value in doing away with some things on the calendar that were age-specific and replacing them with things that were more inclusive.

These very different definitions, while both having their place on the spectrum of intergenerational ministry, found the leaders with differing opinions concerning many ministries around the church where children and adults were both likely to be involved. They were never able to reconcile the differences. If they would have taken the time to lay out clear definitions at the beginning, much of this heartache could have been avoided.

I was on staff with another associate pastor whom I love and respect. I learned the hard way, however, that we had different definitions of intergenerational ministry. She was planning an event with adults and asked our team if we could suggest some people to her for childcare. (As you've read, for a children's leader, this is preferable to being asked to arrange the childcare!) As we were talking about her event, she said, "I want the kids to have some place to go during this prayer meeting so it can truly be intergenerational." That threw me off, as I understood intergenerational to look for ways to *include* kids in the time of prayer. I learned that it was a prayer meeting between many adults across different ages and stages of life, and this pastor wanted the young parents to be free to engage in prayer rather than wrangling their children. She saw intergenerational as the twenty-somethings praying along with the sixty-somethings. She wasn't wrong. Her definition simply didn't go as young as mine. When she said "intergenerational" she meant across generations of adults. When I said it, I meant across all generations.

Intergenerational ministry is not a big, elaborate program to be run. Rather, it's an ethos that permeates throughout everything a church does.

Whatever definition your team lands on, land there together. Any programs, events, or methods will be hard to agree on until everyone is working from the same definition. Have the defining conversation to begin building a philosophy of intergenerational ministry!

NOT A PROGRAM

My philosophy of ministry was shaped by my church growing up. We didn't call it intergenerational ministry, but that's exactly what it was.

While there is definitely some intentionality that needs to be poured into intergenerational and family ministry, let's debunk the scariest part about it right now. Chances are your church is already doing some sort of intergenerational ministry. It's not a big, elaborate program to be run. Rather, it's an ethos that permeates throughout everything a church does.

Consider the moment people walk through the door of your church. Do you have a separate entrance for children only? What about for youth? If you're at a very large church, this may be a yes. But most small to semi-large churches have several entrances and everyone in the family comes in together. Let's say you have a greeter at the west door. We'll call her Karen. A family with a young son comes walking up. Karen opens up the door and greets them all. "Hey, it's the Franklins! We're so glad you're here!" She might shake Mom and Dad's hands, or hand them a bulletin. Let's say Karen bends down and gets right at the level of Jack, their four-year-old. "Hey, Jack," Karen says warmly. "How's that new puppy of yours?" Jack smiles, glad to be known by someone in the church, and begins to open up about his new furry buddy.

> ✹ **A truly intergenerational church finds ways to engage kids, youth, and adults of all ages together in the natural rhythms of life and ministry.**

This is only the tip of the iceberg, but you're witnessing intergenerational ministry as Jack and Karen converse for a moment there on the floor. Karen, your greeter, went out of her way to greet little Jack and make him feel known and welcome. What she did was very simple and required no curriculum or extra programming. Perhaps Karen was just good at it, or perhaps someone trained the greeters well. Simply adding this to the training, asking them to call people, including kids, by name and get down on their level for a brief conversation, is the sort of intentionality that turns a simple church foyer into a hub for intergenerational ministry.

If your church is going to excel at making intergenerational connections, the conversation has to start with the core reasons your faith community exists. Tweaking a program might make that one program intergenerational, but a truly intergenerational church finds ways to engage kids, youth, and adults of all ages together in the natural rhythms of life and ministry.

Simply because kids and adults are occupying the same space does not make ministry intergenerational. There needs to be training and purposeful interactions to make the church a place where everyone feels like they belong. Karen the greeter took her role to the next level when she got down and addressed Jack, asking him about something specific in his life. Not every greeter will know Jack got a new puppy. As I said, Karen may just be really good at her job. For everyone else who needs a little extra boost, a greeter training that invites them to engage with kids in a meaningful way will be important. Even if Karen didn't know Jack got a new puppy, calling him by name, bending down, and asking him something about his life would have done the trick. Her goal was to help Jack feel known, and that's actually pretty easy to do. If she had addressed Jack's parents only, that intergenerational opportunity would have been missed.

> **Instead of looking to add intergenerational ministry to your church, search for ways to adjust current ministries to make them more intergenerational.**

Instead of looking to *add* intergenerational ministry to your church, search for ways to adjust current ministries to make them more intergenerational. Do you have an all-church prayer meeting coming up? Perhaps you could include some tactile prayer stations for people who like to draw or journal their prayers. Or maybe you could provide some Play-Doh to keep little hands busy (which can also help keep little minds engaged). Do you have Wednesday night activities at your church? Consider organizing a quarterly game night where adults and kids play board games together. The sole purpose would be intergenerational connections and relationships. These are small examples that take very little preparation and investment to bring to fruition. If you are ready to take a deeper step into intergenerational ministry, following are some additional examples of all ages sharing together.

THE HOME GROUP

When I was a freshman in college our church began a system of home groups (or life groups), loosely modeled after John Wesley's class meetings. Everyone in a group lived near each other and was challenged to meet regularly for fellowship and intimate sharing. Our group quickly established rhythms for what our life would be like together. We met twice a month. We ate potluck style. We reflected on that week's sermon. We shared intimately about our own lives. We prayed together. This little group quickly became our church within the church. If a family was moving, this was the group that would help them load the truck. If someone was doing home repairs, this was the group to swing a hammer. We became family, and learned to depend on each other.

The group continues to meet to this day. The same rhythms established years ago remain. When I met my wife and started bringing her along, she was received with an abundance of love. They quickly became her people, as much as they were mine. When babies are born, the group makes meals, cleans houses, and babysits older siblings. When the group lost its first member to death, everyone was present and involved in the funeral and grieving process.

I want you to understand how vital these people have become to one another. They exemplify a Wesleyan model of life together. And the kids in the group have been right in the thick of it since the beginning.

When we would gather and share, from the earliest days, the kids would be in the room with us. They would sit in the middle of the circle, playing with toys or coloring with crayons. They were noisy. They asked random questions to their parents. They were messy. But we made a conscious decision not to remove them from this vital part of the group's function. Other home groups from the church used different approaches. Some would hire a teenager from the church to come babysit. Some would take turns each meeting being on child duty, heading down to the basement to make sure everyone stayed alive. Our group decided the kids would join us.

One little girl has been coming since she was a baby. She was familiar with the house and recognized the rhythms. Before she could talk, she would sit amongst those who were sharing and would seem oblivious to what was happening as she colored her picture.

One day, around three years old, she went over to her grandma and whispered, "Grandma, can I share something?" Of course she was encouraged to do so, and from that time on she joined in the sharing during each gathering. The other, younger kids followed suit as they were able.

These kids watched us engage in each other's joys and sorrows. They listened to us cry about lost jobs and celebrate loans going through. They listened as we discussed theology and answered hard questions about evil in the world. If you looked at them, they looked like kids playing with toys. But it was evident in the way they felt comfortable engaging as they got older that they were being shaped by the conversation happening around them.

We didn't force any of them to share. We let them join in at their own pace. But we did always invite them to sit among us. Playing downstairs wasn't an option during this part of our gathering. Everyone joined. Through immersion, they learned what it meant to share.

Imagine if we had taken them out of the room every gathering until they were twelve or so. As twelve-year-olds, they would have entered a foreign environment and would be missing their eleven-year-old friends who were still playing video games downstairs. They would be forced to sit among the adults and listen to everyone talk. They would be asked to share, having never done so in this situation before. They wouldn't understand the value. They wouldn't be part of the story. By allowing them space to be kids but intentionally keeping them close by while we lived our spiritual lives together, it was only natural they would embrace a spiritual life as well. It was all they had ever known. It's what their parents did. It's what other mentors and elders in their lives did. It's what they were going to do as well, by their own choice.

This is intergenerational ministry. It's allowing kids and adults opportunities to engage in the same experiences while still meeting their needs. It's learning from each other. It's not about having things for adults and forcing kids to fit into that mold. It's not about having things for kids and forcing adults to "play down" to the kids' level. It's about being together. It's about allowing space for each to embrace the practices of the other at their own pace. The more we are separated, the less we'll be able to do so.

LOVE IN DEED

A few years ago our staff decided to re-evaluate how our summer mid-week programming looked. Like many churches, participation got pretty low when school let out. It would spike for VBS, then dip for the rest of the summer. We wanted to evaluate if our efforts were best utilized in keeping these programs going through June and July.

Amidst our staff deliberation, we recognized our peoples' need to be together. We decided the five weeks leading up to VBS would be the perfect time to try something new. *Love In Deed* was born.

The Love In Deed program was very simple. The coordinators would line up projects that needed to be done around our city. We worked with individuals, neighborhoods, and our city manager. We found all sorts of cleanup and beautification projects our city needed done, as well as significant cleaning and repair needed for some of our homebound members and our members' neighbors. In place of our traditional mid-week programming, everyone showed up every Wednesday night ready to receive their marching orders and go out into the community to put love into action (to love, in deed).

Here's the kicker: families signed up for these projects together. When one family member signed up, they all did. No regular ministries of the church were open on Wednesday nights during these weeks. If a yard needed to be raked or a house needed to be cleaned, people of all ages were working on the project. Even our babies were involved. In the same way that people took on home projects with their own children in the house, these projects included our littles. If a neighborhood street was being cleaned, you might see a couple strollers being pushed or a toddler putting litter in a trash bag. If a yard was being landscaped, you might see a couple of junior high students taking turns playing with someone's baby or a pre-schooler pulling a rake.

It was more work to have the kids there, yes. But the kids were learning what it looked like to serve their community, and they were participating. A three-year-old can pick up sticks in a yard or help hold a trash bag while dad throws liquor bottles into it. It's messy work, but whole families served together, and whole families were formed together.

In addition to these projects, we adopted two apartment complexes and a park for the summer. We would take teams to these three places to play games with whatever kids were around. After a couple weeks, they began expecting us and we began learning each other's names. We advertised our VBS and when that week came we ran buses to the locations, following necessary safety procedures, bringing lots of kids who wouldn't have come otherwise. When they came to VBS, they saw the familiar faces of adults, kids, and teens that had been playing with them the previous weeks, since all generations were involved.

Love In Deed was a success. It became the church's summer ministry program for years to follow. People learned to serve together. People learned to do the messy work of living as a family, not just enduring in it, but thriving!

FAMILY WORSHIP: WHY?

How often are kids in service with their families at your church? Every week? Once a month? Once a quarter? Twice a year? Never? I know different churches that could answer yes to each of these options, respectively. It's understandable that family worship can be overwhelming to some pastors. There are so many practical questions to answer: How do we engage the kids in a long service without making it a circus? How do we engage the adults without completely losing the kids? How often should we do it? It's such a hassle, should we even do it at all?

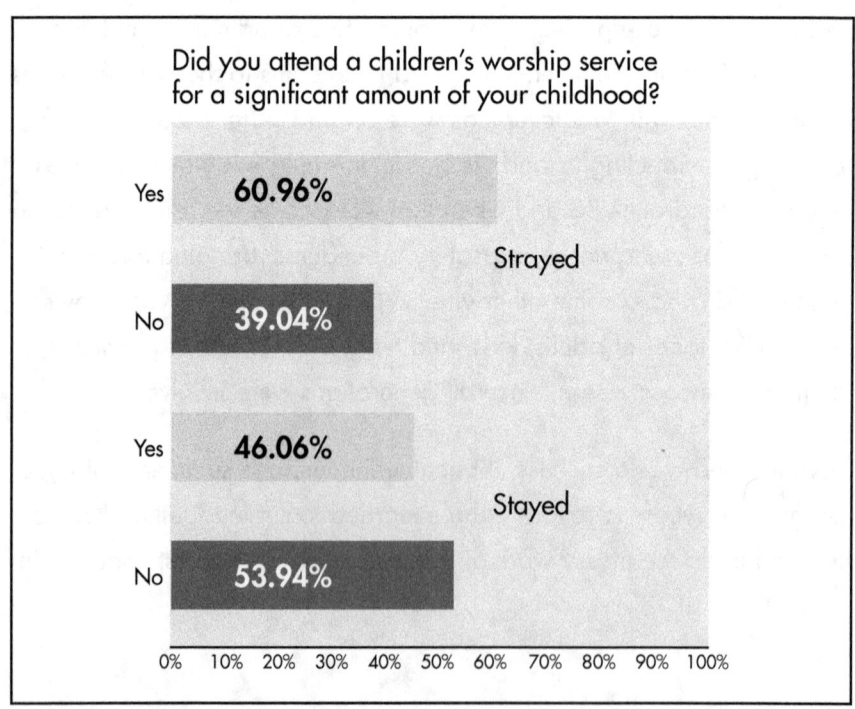

Sometimes the decision to move to intergenerational worship isn't a popular one. The kids complain about it because they love going to kids' worship. The adults complain about it because they don't get a break from their kids. It can feel like a no-win. Why should we bother?

Dr. Steve Parr, longtime pastor and church growth expert, and Dr. Tom Crites, research specialist, took a survey of young adults (aged twenty-five to forty years) who grew up in the church. Their purpose was to understand why people stayed in the church, and why people strayed from the church. Parr and Crites wrote a book about their research called *Why They Stay*. One question the authors asked respondents was how often they worshiped as a child with their parents, as opposed to being separated into a kid-specific worship environment. The results were fascinating. "Young adults who attended worship services that separated them from their parents when they were children were 38% more likely to have strayed as a young adult than those who were not in separate services."[1] There is great value to having kids worship alongside the rest of the church. Similar to our home group, if "adult worship" or "big church" is unfamiliar to kids, when they become teenagers and are suddenly dropped into this new life, they won't know what to do with it. The sanctuary won't be their sanctuary. The pastor won't be their pastor. The music won't be their music. It will be foreign. Crites and Parr go on, "What is the result if you place a child for several years (which is most of their life if they are under eleven years of age) in a high-energy, though well-meaning, children's worship service and then transition them to the adult worship service as an adolescent? To be blunt, in their mind you have moved them from an interesting experience to a very boring experience."[2] Chances are, some will get lost who aren't able to assimilate.

The case for family worship is not just about a child's transition to the teenage years, though. Kids need to see leaders in the church and mentors in their lives worshiping Jesus. In the children's ministry area, all the adults are there to serve the kids. Children don't think abstractly enough to understand this as an act of worship for those adults, even though it is. Children come to church and see lots of adults who are there to help them learn, grow, and have fun. They can begin to view church as "all about me" when they get there and every adult's job seems to be attending to their individual needs. Kids need to recognize the church as a place of worship for all generations!

Adults can learn from children. When my daughters were young they would dance in the aisles during the worship music. Yes, it was super cute, but it was also a good lesson for all of us. These kids worshiped with complete abandon. They didn't care who was watching or what anyone was thinking. We were singing to Jesus. They didn't know the words so they worshiped with their whole selves, spinning, swaying, and clapping. While this was mostly met with approval, I did get a couple of critical looks from adults who thought I should keep a tighter rein on my children. These adults are likely of the same breed who told me not to run in the church out of respect for God's house when I was a kid. I honestly thought it was a sin to run in church until I was an older teenager and realized how ridiculous that sounded. I don't think God cares if we run in church. I also think he's delighted by a two-year-old dancing in the aisle during worship. As congregants looked on, I received many words of blessing. "Your daughters really know how to worship. They're teaching me!" There is no pretense with kids. We can learn from them.

Kids can also learn to worship from us. I have a picture of my daughter standing in the aisle with her hand in the air during a song. I was watching her closely. She was dancing, did a little twirl, and landed facing a woman across the aisle. The woman had her eyes closed and her hand up. It wasn't a woman we knew particularly well. She was simply a dear old saint of the church. My daughter watched her curiously for a moment before turning to face the platform and glancing back at the woman. My daughter then assumed the same posture as the worshiper, lifting her hand in the air and closing her eyes. This woman was shaping how my daughter engaged in worship in that space. I thanked her later.

When we talk about family worship with our congregants, it's important to avoid language that perpetuates barriers between the generations. Avoid saying things like, "Kids are joining us for *our* worship service today" or "The kids don't have *their* service today." Calling a worship service "ours" or "theirs" widens the gap. Children should not feel like they're joining someone else's worship. Rather, use inclusive language that says "this service, this church, these songs, these scriptures, these movements, these sacraments . . . they belong to all of us." Let us take care to be sure our language doesn't make anyone feel like an outsider or guest.

Family worship, with all ages together, will benefit your church greatly if it happens regularly. There is definitely still a need for kids and adults to learn in age-appropriate spaces and times, but being segregated should not be the only way they spend their time at church. Bringing the generations together allows them to shape one another.

FAMILY WORSHIP: PREACHING

"Daddy, what's a hooker?" is not the question you want the ten-year-old in the room asking during the service. It was family worship Sunday, which happened once a month at this church. The lead pastor was excited to have family worship but could have used some coaching regarding content rating on these weeks. He told an important story with a prostitute as the main character. After saying the word "hooker," one particular preteen turned to her dad and offered this inquiry. I doubt church leadership wants parents coming up after a service complaining that the material was too PG-13 for their kids. Another pastor told a story of a brutal murder, including some very graphic details, to help hammer home a point she was making. I'm not sure if parents in the room will ever remember the point of the story, but they will remember the crisis care they had to offer to their children on the drive home!

While keeping the content appropriate and PG rated, there are several simple ways to engage kids in a sermon. This may take some collaboration between the preaching pastor and the children's team. First, be aware of the length. People will be especially appreciative of this family worship Sunday when the kids are in the room. If the sermon is more than twenty minutes on that Sunday, consider finding a way to break it up in the middle. Maybe show a video ten minutes in, tell a funny story, sing a song, or use an object lesson or visual aid. These techniques can offer a reprieve to short attention spans.

Second, involve a child in the sermon's story. I watched a lead pastor masterfully pull this from his family worship arsenal many times. Early in his sermon, he would pull a child (who had some prior warning) on the platform to help him with a lesson. It might have been something very simple like counting some pennies and putting them in a piggy bank before he told the story of the widow and her coins. He would joke with the child, and they would laugh together as they interacted for a few moments before the child headed back to his seat and the pastor would launch into the rest of the sermon. When the kid was on the platform, every other kid in the room was at full attention. Kids love watching other kids. It doesn't have to be anything elaborate. A simple visual and some playful banter goes a long way in helping other kids to engage.

Other ways to involve kids in presentations from the front might be to simply tell a story about a kid. Make the story come to life with lots of details and descriptions so all the kids in the room can visualize and follow along. Even better, if possible, tell a story about a child in your church. (Get permission first.) Lift them up and praise them for something they've done from which we could all learn. Another technique is to use videos with kids in them.

Third, give kids something to do. Hand out pieces of paper and challenge everyone in the room to draw something they hear in the sermon. Then, afterward, offer to hang up the drawings for everyone to see. Maybe they draw Jericho with the wall around it, or Jesus in the upper room with his disciples, or the Good Samaritan on the road, or whatever else might be happening in your story. Challenge them to listen closely so they know what details to include. Give clues in the sermon about things that might need to be added to the drawing.

FAMILY WORSHIP: WIGGLES AND WHISPERS

You can really help parents feel comfortable in family worship by naming some things that could be stressors and giving space for them. A speech I often give on family worship Sunday sounds something like this:

> Today is family worship Sunday. We believe there is value in the whole church worshiping together, with no generational lines drawn. Kids aren't in here today because we didn't have anyone to lead them, or because we're giving the children's ministry staff a break. Kids, you're with your whole church family today because we belong together! We have an opportunity to join together in worship, to learn from one another, to be the church together!
>
> We recognize that not everyone worships in the same way. Some people, especially smaller people, move around a lot. They crinkle paper and snack wrappers, turn around in the pew, and ask lots of questions. We welcome wiggles and whispers in worship! Please do not feel uncomfortable if there's extra noise coming from your pew. We knew that would happen when we planned family wor-

ship! Actually, we're even excited about it! Wiggles and whispers mean the church is alive and growing. We're thrilled to be together as one body today!"

SILO BUSTING

Another aspect of intergenerational ministry takes place in the church office. Keeping lines of communication open between different ministry areas is vital. How often are your children's leader and your young adult leader working together? Whether you're in a church large enough to have a paid staff position for each, or you're in a smaller church where both are led by volunteers, they should be sitting around the same table semi-regularly to exchange ideas and collaborate. Many young adults in the church have children, and they are centering their lives around their young family. Why would we send two separate ministers from two separate areas into these families' lives without inviting these ministers to work together? Your young adult pastor/leader should be very well versed in what's happening in children's ministry at your church. She should know the events, the ethos, the Sunday morning schedule, how families could learn more, and how adults could get involved as volunteers. Adults with kids are looking for ways to connect to children's ministry. When we send young adult, discipleship, or senior pastors to build relationships with these families, we should equip these leaders to talk about children's ministry!

In the same way, the children's leader is often so wrapped up in the world of children's ministry, sometimes never leaving the basement, that he knows very little about what goes on in the world of young adults. A primary point of his ministry will be to parents, but he can't really speak about ministries that are geared toward them because he lives in his world of construction paper and squirrel puppets. The children's leader and young adult leader should be sitting down regularly, along with the lead pastor, and talking about what's going on in ministry. If there is a children's ministry event that involves the parents, perhaps the young adult leader could be there. Don't miss those opportunities to connect. Break down the silos. Get on the same page. Work together. This offers a much more strategic approach to connecting across the generations.

✷ 6 ✷
A SAFE PLACE

This stuff is hard to talk about, and I wish it weren't necessary. I know many of us look fondly back on our days growing up in the church and can't understand "where it all went wrong." However, it's important that churches be proactive about the issues in this chapter. The end goal is a safe place for our kids, our volunteers, and our staff.

Real-world example 1: a pastor was accused of numerous sexual crimes against young girls, getting caught in situation after situation where he was alone with them. He was well connected within his local church, an affiliated university, and the community.

Real-world example 2: a children's ministry volunteer was arrested in his home for possession of child pornography.

Real-world example 3: a young girl told her pastor that her father was molesting her. It was happening every time she visited her dad, who was divorced from her mother but had regular visitation rights. The pastor was required by state law to report what he was told, but he neglected to do so. Not only did he fail to report to the proper law enforcement authorities, but he also neglected to tell the mother or anyone else. The child went on being molested for nearly two more years before she finally told her mother, who put a stop to it and sued the church.

> ☀ **Safety has to be on our radar, no matter our church size.**

Each of these incidents is so sad. Unfortunately, it's not hard to find other examples. As leaders in our churches, it is imperative that we ask the following questions: How safe is our church for both children and volunteers? How well-screened are our volunteers? How are we helping parents *know* their church is safe? Each of these above stories was in the news and very public information. Why would a savvy parent, who is aware of what has happened in other churches, feel confident dropping a child off in your church?

Children's leaders are responsible for creating safe environments for everyone involved; this can be a heavy task. The more the whole staff, church board, and leadership teams understand about safety in the church, the better equipped everyone will be to affix and enforce safety procedures.

According to one molestation prevention study, reported by Religion News, only 3% of sexual offenders have a chance of getting caught.

In another study, every single offender who was interviewed had been previously turned in by an abused child and each report had been ignored. The first study also revealed that 93% of abusers consider themselves religious.[1] This means there is a very large chance that abusers are turning up at our churches. We have an opportunity to turn some of these statistics around through awareness and prevention. Safety has to be on our radar, no matter our church size.

"We have a small church and everyone knows everyone." Unfortunately, this mindset isn't valid anymore. There are no excuses for not having safety policies in place and following them to the letter. They might make things more difficult or cumbersome at times, but the protection from what could happen far outweighs the inconvenience. Let's look at some ways your church can and must be a safe place for everyone in children's ministry—the kids and adults alike.

WRITTEN POLICY

Ground zero for church safety is a written policy and procedure manual concerning both rules and best practices. You don't have to reinvent the wheel to get your policy written. If you are a smaller church, chances are there's a larger church within your denomination, or right around the corner, that would be willing to share their written policies and procedures with you. Not everything will apply, but you'll be tweaking language to fit your context rather than writing it from scratch.

In my experience with creating safeguards for a large church, policies and procedures were not included in the manual without first being reviewed by an attorney. Our manual, therefore, was legally strong and written with the appropriate language to protect children, volunteers, and leadership. This is another reason to use the larger churches around you as a resource for your own manual. Take advantage of a church's generosity that has been able to pay a legal mind to fine-tune their verbiage. If you are that larger church, don't write your policy without the necessary input of an attorney.

If you're writing a policy in-house, or adapting someone else's, establish a policy and procedure team from your church. This team will be responsible for the writing and annual upkeep of the policies. Members should include your children's leader and a core volunteer, your youth leader and a core volunteer, then others in your church who will ask necessary questions and help the team think all the way through each policy. If there is a police officer, school counselor, psychologist, teacher, nurse, or human resources expert in your congregation, consider adding that person to the team. Each of these will bring a different and important perspective to your discussion. It is best if not everyone on the team works in ministries to children or youth, so an outside perspective is always being offered.

A strong policy on safety should include things like classroom ratios, bathroom procedures, reporting procedures, fire and active shooter procedures, appropriate discipline measures, special policies for different age levels, special policies for recurring events, general conduct, overnight event procedures, and volunteer expectations concerning inappropriate behavior at and away from church.

When you have a written policy, you can make a particular procedure the bad guy in uncomfortable situations. Rather than having to pull a volunteer aside and say, "I'd really like you to stop doing _____," you can pull a volunteer aside and say, "Hey, I just want to remind you what it says in our policy and procedure manual about _____." Reference the manual often. Make it clear that leaders know the content very well and that the policy manual has a constant presence in the lens through which leadership is viewing ministry. Good policies and procedures help mitigate the fear that something terrible might happen at your church, especially if all volunteers are well-acquainted with it.

It is important to get the written policy in the hands of every volunteer and leader in your church. Include a page in the policy that must be signed by them, stating they've read the policy and will comply with it. This will help protect the church if something does happen (showing that all volunteers were aware of all policies), but even more important it forces volunteers to read the policy. It's also a good idea to require a newly signed page to be turned in at regular intervals (maybe every other year) so you know volunteers and other leaders are re-reading the policy. Keep copies of it for quick reference in volunteer hangout spaces. All church staff, board, deacons, elders, ushers, and greeters should know the policy and have a signed copy on file. This is important for the church's protection and the children's protection.

REPORTING

Are your pastors mandated reporters, according to your state's law? A mandated reporter is legally responsible for reporting abuse, be it suspected or disclosed, to authorities. Some states have clergy listed specifically. Some states include any professional working with children. You need to know the mandatory reporting laws in your state, and what the necessary procedures are.

Even if you aren't a mandated reporter, it's important to know what you will do if you learn about or suspect abuse. Reporting doesn't automatically mean someone is going to jail or children are being taken away. It is important, however, that we as leaders do not bear the burden to make the distinction between what is abuse and what is not. There are professionals whose job it is to do just that.

If you are a mandated reporter, you have a legal obligation to report. You don't get to decide. Choosing not to report on a situation that surfaces with real abuse can involve surrendering your credentials or facing legal consequences. If you are not a mandated reporter by your state's standards, it will be important to approach the ethical dilemma of your responsibility before a situation arises.

TRAINING

Included in your training structure (which we discussed in chapter 3) should be information on safety and abuse awareness.

There are many systems available online that handle safety training in video form. Some allow you to track what training videos your volunteers have watched so you can track their progress. If you think your people would better respond to a live event, invite someone from your local police department or child services to come for a special volunteer training. Your group needs to know what signs of abuse to look and listen for in their conversations with kids. They need to be empowered to ask the right questions and know the procedure if reporting is necessary. Most abuse awareness also helps to equip adults to look for signs of grooming (inappropriately breaking down defenses) in potential abusers, as well as other red flags. This is heavy subject matter, but your volunteers will walk away feeling empowered and prepared to care for your church's kids in new ways.

Such trainings need to happen regularly, perhaps bi-annually. A volunteer should revisit the abuse awareness training and re-read the policy and procedure manual. It sounds like a lot, but it requires only two to three hours every other year. Not an overwhelming investment for the safety of kids in your church.

BACKGROUND CHECKS

"Do you need to have my social security number for the background check you keep on file?" one volunteer asked me. I confirmed that we did, based on the system we were using. "Then I'm sorry but I won't submit to a background check. I'm very careful with my social security number."

This volunteer wasn't taking my request lightly. He had been working with kids for a couple years and was willing to continue volunteering. He was a good volunteer, and everyone in children's ministry knows it seems to be harder to get men to volunteer. I was in a quandary. He had a legitimate reason, in his mind, for not wanting to have his information in our file cabinet. I had a legitimate reason for asking him for it. I went back and forth on what I was going to do for some time until I got some advice from another pastor at a neighboring church. "What's more important? Having this one person continue to volunteer or having all of your volunteers in compliance with your safety procedures if something happens?"

The answer was obvious. The volunteer was very understanding of my reasoning when I asked him one last time for a background check form. He respectfully declined and was removed from my volunteer list.

Getting and keeping volunteers is really hard, and I don't like to decline anyone. Even more, this was a good dad in our church, a strong male presence and role model. Chances are, nothing was ever going to happen. But if something ever did, I would not be able to say to the church board, or my district denominational leadership, or a judge, or a child's parents that I did *everything in my power* to make sure my whole team was in compliance with our safety procedures.

It's that important.

Background checks are another necessary piece to the safety puzzle. The same list of people who should have a signed page from your policy and procedure manual on file, should also have a background check on file. Default to being over-prepared.

Perhaps you are in a small church. It might seem silly to do a background check on Edna Green who has been teaching Sunday school since the moon landing. And, background checks are in no way a catch-all. In all three of the case studies at the beginning of this chapter, a background check would have done no good. None of the offenders had prior arrests or convictions.

Background checks are a deterrent. They are another barrier to keep potentially harmful people out of your ministry volunteer system. Background checks say, "We pay attention to child safety at this church." If some unsavory-type person did want to get involved with kids at a church, it would be much more inviting to do so at a church that didn't do background checks on volunteers.

MORE THAN BACKGROUND CHECKS

Other policies like abuse awareness trainings and mandatory reporting must be in your manual precisely because background checks are insufficient. Although they are necessary, your commitment to safety cannot end there.

Accountability should permeate your church culture. Applying to every possible situation, no adult, paid or volunteer, should find himself or herself alone with a child. All three incidents we cited at the beginning of this chapter could have been avoided if this policy had been followed. In all three examples, if the necessary steps had been taken to see that no adult was ever one-on-one with a kid, lots of kids would have been saved from devastating situations. Even with the pastor who failed to report, if there had been another adult in the room, he would have had another level of accountability to follow his mandatory duty.

Your policy must include a clear statement that no adult can be alone with a child. There should always be at least two adults in a room with kids. This must be followed at Vacation Bible School, at church camp, at retreats and lock-ins, as well as normal Sunday and Wednesday routines. Yes, it makes things more difficult, but once again, the safe environment far outweighs the inconvenience.

A few years ago at my church a little girl told her mom on a Sunday afternoon that a man had shown her pornographic images on his phone. This was one of the biggest scares I've ever walked through in my ministry. Authorities got involved: sheriff's department, child services. We immediately went on the hunt to figure out who she was talking about and when and where it could have happened. We had a strong policy in place that was signed by every volunteer. We were as covered as we knew how to be.

Our policy of a minimum of two adults in every classroom came through for us. Through the investigation, including, but not limited to, interviews with other volunteers and a tireless reviewing of security footage (which covered hallways) it was determined that this little girl was never alone with any adults on the Sunday in question. As a matter of fact, the classroom she was in had four adults present. After further discussion with the police, it was concluded that she was likely referring to a different adult at a different time and place, and was reporting it to her mom for the first time that Sunday.

First, we were so sad that this little girl had endured any of this. Second, we were glad she was talking with her mom and they had an opportunity to deal with this abuse. Third, we were glad we had policies in place that kept both her and our volunteers safe.

That particular instance gave our committee an opportunity to revisit the manual. We realized that volunteers had their phones with them most of the time, which could create the opportunity to pull them out and show inappropriate content. It was unlikely to happen, but it needed to be addressed. It was not uncommon for a volunteer to show pictures of their puppy or family to kids, or to take a selfie with the preteens, or to show a video for class. We included language in our best practices about phones staying in pockets and purses during ministry hours, and only using them for videos or other classroom resources if they're being shown to the whole group at once. Again, further accountability. This is an example of the necessity of revisiting the policy regularly.

REASSURING PARENTS

Having necessary policies and procedures in place go a long way in helping parents know you've created a very safe environment for their kids. The parents who have been at your church forever, or have even grown up there themselves, aren't necessarily your target audience here. It's equally as important to keep their kids safe, but likely these parents already feel very comfortable and know all the volunteers personally. However, if you want your church to be ready for guests, helping parents feel reassured about their kids' safety is a must.

☀ Parents will appreciate how prepared you are to keep their kids safe.

In the interests of transparency, make your policy available for parents to read. Perhaps someone can post it on your church's website. Maybe you can send it out in PDF form once a year in an email. Maybe you include a copy of it in new parent packets after they've visited a couple times. Regardless of how you distribute them, the policies should be highly visible. They are not meant to scare anyone; in fact, they will have the opposite effect! Parents will appreciate how prepared you are to keep their kids safe. They will appreciate the full disclosure of the procedures and knowing everything a volunteer must do and know to be allowed to work with kids. The policy and procedure manual says to guests and regulars alike, "We're ready for your kids!"

Another way to reassure parents is to have your volunteers wear nametags. Again, I know this feels silly if you're in a small church and everyone already knows each other, but nametags carry a two-fold purpose. First, new parents feel more comfortable knowing more about the people who will be caring for their children. They're not encountering nameless strangers. They're meeting Tom. They're meeting Stacy. Like the background check is an extra barrier to predators, the nametag is an extra extension of welcome to guests. Second, the nametag says you belong there. If all volunteers are required to wear nametags, it's easy to spot people hanging out near the kids' area who aren't wearing one. This helps with security purposes. Either you're a parent dropping your kids off, or you're wearing a nametag that announces to the church that you work with kids. This is an extra layer of protection.

An additional presence in the hallway also helps reassure parents. Don't let them get deep into your children's ministry area for drop-off without encountering someone who is specifically placed to make them feel welcome and safe. This person helps the parents to be properly greeted and directed, and it reassures them that someone is watching this hall and sees everyone coming in and out. A hallway greeter is as much a security role as it is a position of hospitality.

A good idea is to invite someone with fresh eyes to walk through your children's area. Invite a person from a neighboring church to come as a "secret shopper" and see what sort of experience they have. You can trade secret shoppers with the church, so you both benefit from the experiment. From your secret shoppers, you may be able to glean some things that will help guests feel reassured and safe. (As an aside, you'll also be able to find out what systems at your church might be confusing or overwhelming, how user-friendly your website is, how welcomed guests felt by greeters, etc.) Give your shoppers a list of questions ahead of time, so they know what interactions they need to have and what sort of report you'll be expecting. This is a great way to figure out how guests see your church in general, but especially how safe they feel your children's ministry is.

✸ 7 ✸
MAKE SPACE

In our survey of children's leaders, there were a few things that felt like a continual struggle for many. All of these came back to the same thing: space. There are a couple specific areas of ministry in which children's leaders often feel like they're jockeying for space, fighting an uphill battle for a little room. In this final chapter, let's take a look at where children's ministry could use a little space to thrive.

PHYSICAL SPACE

We were nearing the response time in what was turning out to be a fantastic Advent children's worship service. Sure our platform was nicely decorated, and the lighting was just right, but more importantly the kids really connected with the music that Sunday and were attentive to the preaching. I was landing the plane in preparation to direct the kids to Advent-themed prayer stations. From our seats we would move to the stations where we were going to have ten minutes of quiet prayer as kids engaged by writing, reading, and building. I closed the sermon and invited the kids to join in a time of prayer. They got up from their seats as soft music began to play and made their way to the tables set up around the room. It was a quiet, worshipful atmosphere.

Then came the coffee cart.

Clang! Clink! Crack! *Whisper* *Whisper* The church's kitchen was attached to our children's sanctuary and supplies were kept in the kitchen for many Sunday school classes' morning caffeine fix. No judgment from me, there. I was riding my second cup of coffee that morning. The cart, however, squeaked and squealed with a prodigious cry that seemed to say, "Stop pushing me! It hurts!" It's okay, though, because the bumps and clinks from the cups and carafes on the cart as it went over door transitions and navigated around tables and chairs offered the necessary din to drown out the poor, desperate wheels on the bottom. The people pushing the cart were doing their best to keep it quiet. Sometimes they would give each other advice pertaining to guiding the cart through the obstacle course. Sometimes they would laugh nervously at the awkwardness when a hundred small heads would turn and look at the noise. Sometimes these small heads would look up from prayer stations. Sometimes they would turn in their seats to watch the commotion. It seemed that the coffee cart always came by right around the time we were bringing the service to a close, usually leading up to prayer or attempting to bring home a point. The coffee cart was not my friend.

We also had the misfortune of being in a room that had outside entrances along one wall, and our platform offered a shortcut, if one were to choose, to skip a little walking and make it straight to the main foyer. I cannot count the times people would come in the doors and walk across the platform while I or someone on our team was preaching or leading worship, just for a shortcut to the foyer.

We were in a shared space. It was a beautiful space, with natural lighting, a decent sound system, and plenty of room. It's a space many children's leaders would pine for. We were blessed to have it. I simply want to use these stories of sharing space to help us all understand where many children's leaders are coming from.

One children's leader, in a church that meets in an elementary school, told me some of the classrooms have sinks and some do not. The classroom designated for kids' worship has a sink in the back. It was nice to get one with a sink, in case there are crafts or stations that require some messy cleanup. However, since the classroom next door, where adults meet for Sunday school, doesn't have a sink, adults will come to the children's worship space to use the sink. The result is that the children's leader preaches while coffee cups are being washed in the back of the room.

One children's leader describes his shared space as a room that has other staff members' offices connected to it. Staff members will quietly come in to their offices, but then people will come to chat with them, standing in doorways and talking casually during kids' worship.

Shared space is a reality for many of our churches. I've had shared children's space at each of the churches at which I've been on staff.

In our survey of children's leaders, nearly 60% share their space with other ministries in the church either on Sundays or throughout the week. Sometimes they share their space with adult Sunday school classes that also meet that morning, or they share it with mid-week programming. Sometimes, "sharing" takes on a different meaning, like with one leader who said their space "is not shared but is sometimes used as a dumping ground for storage."

Let's look again into the inner monologue of the children's leader. This may be what many of them want to say but don't feel like they'd ever be allowed to say.

"Imagine if we stored our supplies in a closet right off the back of the sanctuary. It's 10:55 and the lead pastor is wrapping up the sermon when one of us walks in with a volunteer, talking quietly about what we need to get. We open up the closet, load our cart with stuff, and noisily make our way out the back of the sanctuary. At first it was a mild distraction, but by the time the cart starts squealing and we drop a few chenille stems and have to bend over and pick them up while giggling nervously, it becomes a full-on diversion. Most heads are turned to watch the commotion and the preacher has lost the attention of the congregation as the carefully crafted sermon was coming in for a landing. Can you imagine? Welcome to our world!"

Or . . .

"Imagine that the lead pastor gets to church early on Sunday and turns on the lights of the sanctuary to see a bunch of leftover fruit snacks and board games from our preteen event Friday night. We needed it out of our space for Sunday morning so we quickly tossed it on a table in the back of the sanctuary to be dealt with later. Now there's scrambling to find a place for this mess so the space is prepared Sunday as it should be."

THE SANCTUARY

Obviously those are extreme examples that likely won't happen to our main worship spaces. However, these kinds of things happen in children's worship spaces all the time. Because they are shared spaces, they get used for temporary storage, are re-designed without the input of the children's leader, or can be invaded during worship because others need to use them for their other functions (like coffee cart keeping).

☀ Help your children's leader design and lead worship in a sacred space.

The best way to combat these frustrations is to change our language in terms of the way we talk about the children's space. Specifically, use the word "sanctuary." In kids' worship we find liturgies, worship music, corporate prayer, preaching, response, and sending. These are the elements of the worship service that are taking place upstairs, down the hall, or across the parking lot in the "main" or "big" sanctuary. It will help everyone in the church begin to value the children's worship space if we begin using proper language and call it a sanctuary. Even if your children's worship has a specific name—Kids in the House, Hiz Kidz, or Worship Rock Central—use language that suggests that worship takes place in a sanctuary. Sanctuaries aren't dumping grounds for event gear overflow. Sanctuaries aren't prep spaces for other happenings in the church. Sanctuaries are sacred spaces. Help your children's leader design and lead worship in a sacred space. Even if it's a shared space, work on coordinating schedules and maintenance in a way that respects the space when it has been set aside as a sanctuary.

One large church has a beautiful designated children's space. The room is designed theater-style with built-in floor risers and chairs in neat rows. Intelligent lights are suspended from the ceiling with a paid media tech designated to run their sound, lights, and video each Sunday. The platform design is contemporary and eye-catching. There are permanent prayer stations all around the room that never need to be torn down because the space belongs to children's ministry and children's ministry alone. It was a dream for most children's leaders.

There is a children's worship space that is right off the kitchen, in the basement fellowship hall of a small, country church. Each week there are both children and adult Sunday school classes that meet in the adjoining rooms. The kitchen is a gathering place for several who love to drink coffee and share informal conversation on Sunday mornings. There is a flurry of activity in the space, and only some of it belongs to children's ministry. Anytime there is a potluck after church, kids' worship is either moved or cancelled to make space for those who will be putting together the meal during the service time.

These are two very different settings for children's worship. What's important to remember, though, is that they are both sanctuaries. Each week, in each space, kids hear about Jesus from passionate leaders who have dedicated their lives to the spiritual development of kids in the church. These leaders read the text and do the exegetical work in preparation to bring a message of love and hope to kids who need to hear it. One space is beautiful, set aside for this kind of worship. One space has multiple functions, even within a single Sunday morning. Both, though, are sanctuaries. Both are sacred spaces. Both need the language and the commitment to be treated as such.

Along with this language change, leaders can be more intentional about the words used when talking about children's ministry. When kids are dismissed to go to kids' worship, or when they're welcomed on a family worship Sunday, don't say, "Hope you have fun!" That's what you say when a kid is going outside to play, or over to a friend's house. If the kids are heading to a sacred space to continue in worship, or if they've joined the rest of the church in an intergenerational sacred space, what would you say instead? Maybe consider a word of blessing that could be spoken over kids. Perhaps consider language that would charge them to grow, explore, and be transformed. It's okay if children's worship is fun, but that's not the point! Whatever you hope for your adults in a regular worship service, plan to offer those words of encouragement and blessing to kids as they prepare for worship, whether that's from the platform or a conversation in the hallway.

SPACE IN THE BUDGET

In our survey, we asked children's leaders how they felt like their church board could be most supportive of their work. The answer most often given had to do with finances. Either they were very appreciative of their board approving a workable budget, or they were really wishing their board would. In the minds of many of those surveyed, support equals budget.

We all know that every church ministry likely needs and wants a bigger budget. I've not been at a church where budget wasn't perpetually on the minds of the lay leadership and the staff. Money certainly presents an opportunity for people to be faithful, but I think we would all prefer it if we didn't need it at all. But we do.

Kids have no money of their own. They don't have jobs or the option to get jobs. Many of them haven't started receiving allowance yet, or if they do it's very small. Therefore, unlike areas of ministry with adults, kids can't be expected to pay for things themselves. Also, since kids can't drive, there is plenty of money to be spent on them in transportation alone. If you're a parent, you know how expensive kids' lives are. Essentially, ministry to both children and youth is so expensive because kids and teens can't be asked to financially contribute much themselves.

Children's ministry budgets also tend to need a little inflation for the sake of classroom activities. There are innumerable crafts that come along with kids' worship, especially in early childhood. Kids are often encouraged to learn with their hands. Actually, adults can benefit from this too, but somehow we've slowly weeded active learning out as kids have gotten older so that by the time they're adults they are expected to sit and listen with their hands folded neatly in their laps. (My wife and I never got this memo, and we doodle furiously during the sermon. Maybe it's because of our work with children for so many years.) Since it's still very acceptable for kids, however, plenty of ministry dollars are spent on crayons, markers, and those little fluffy pom-poms you get at craft stores. Oh, and glitter. Children's curriculum also often comes with many cutouts, take-home sheets, and extra craft projects. High-quality curriculum can be very expensive, but that quality really matters (more about this shortly).

Considering the tactile nature of teaching children, along with the fact that kids cannot contribute financially to any ongoing or event-driven ministries put together for them, a robust budget is a great way to a children's leader's heart. It can be read in the responses of those surveyed.

Q: In what ways do you feel like your church board is most supportive of children's ministry?

A: "By financially supporting."

A: "Budget."

A: "Approving a workable budget."

A: "Budget speaks volumes."

A: "FUNDS."

Those responses are from the very first page of the survey answers, and that's not all of them:

A: "They approve budget that is needed for the children's ministry."

A: "They approve my budget every single year!"

A: "Providing funds to keep children safe."

A: "We have a budget."

This last person even recognizes the fact that having a budget is more than some children's ministries can say. In our question specifically about children's ministry budget, there were several answers that indicated that their budget is less than 3% of the church's overall budget.

In general, it should be standard operating procedure to have a budget in place for each ministry. This may seem like an obvious statement, but I've been in situations and even received survey feedback that has shown no ministry budgets. Instead, everything operates on an as-needed basis. In times of financial strife, this is understandable. When there isn't much money, it should go to the ministries that most need it at the time. Budgets are fluid. They're suggestions based on expected giving. However, whenever possible, allowing children's leaders the opportunity to work from a budget gives them autonomy, ownership over their area of ministry, and a sense of trust that they'll make the right decisions.

When you plan your yearly budgeting, it's important to avoid the temptation to tie up all your funds in events. Make sure there is space for relationships and investment in kids, parents, and volunteers. While the children's leader may not get to come up with the numbers for the budget, perhaps they could have significant input creating the line items that add up to the final number.

SPACE IN CURRICULUM

There are about seventy billion children's ministry curricula out there. (I checked.) Where should a children's leader even start when trying to choose a curriculum? Should we look at the free stuff since our budget is small? Do we use our denomination's curriculum, so we know it complies to our doctrine? Should we choose a highly interactive curriculum that features lots of crafts and video content? What outcomes are we trying to achieve? In what way can a curriculum pick up the slack where I fall short? There are so many questions.

☀ There is no curriculum that can be purchased that makes up for genuine relationships built between kids and their adult mentors.

Curriculum can help kids engage with the story. A great children's leader doesn't have to be a dynamic storyteller and charismatic personality. They must first love the kids and care about their holistic development. There is no curriculum that can be purchased that makes up for genuine relationships built between kids and their adult mentors. A children's leader must be able to build these relationships, or be surrounded by people who can. However, if a children's leader or Sunday school teacher is *not* a dynamic storyteller and presenter of the gospel, the right curriculum can be a great way to make up for some of that skill set.

A high-quality curriculum will offer built-in ways to tell stories and engage kids in the Word. Many of them will offer some sort of host with a dynamic personality, someone with whom the kids can engage, who is funny and genuine. The kids will look forward to interacting with the host, be it a cartoon character on the page or a puppet on a screen, each week. Not every children's ministry leader or volunteer is an engaging storyteller. That's one reason why curriculum is so important.

Curriculum can provide a strong pedagogy. Not everyone teaching Sunday school is a trained elementary school teacher. You may invite a senior in high school to teach a class for you, or a CPA, or a welder. A high-quality curriculum can provide teaching methods, classroom management systems, and continued ways to engage in the story beyond Sunday morning. Some curricula even offer teacher trainings on video, in print, or live. The right curriculum can develop and equip teachers.

Curriculum can shape theology. If your children's leader is trained in your faith tradition, with a strong grasp on your doctrines and a great eye for catching things in curriculum that may not line up with your belief structure, then you can feel confident with your leader going out into the world and choosing the right curriculum. If a children's leader lacks this training or doesn't feel confident to make this decision, a lead pastor can assume that role as resident theologian to help with curriculum vetting. Essentially, someone needs to be the theological gatekeeper to ensure the curriculum chosen fits.

Curriculum can provide steadiness in a crazy world. For the kids who move from teacher to teacher throughout the years, or if a church has a fair amount of teacher turnover, curriculum can be the constant that anchors kids into routine and common language. If there's a substitute teacher one week, or if the children's leader is called to another church, or if kids are nervous about graduating to the next grade level, curriculum can provide those characters, classroom structures, and recognizable graphics and styles that keep things familiar.

Curriculum can fill in the gaps where the leader lacks skills or confidence. Perhaps the leader is very comfortable leading kids in worship through song but is not a great storyteller. Find a curriculum where the story is told through video or is mapped out very carefully through melodrama or other simple methods. Perhaps the leader is a great storyteller but struggles with choosing and leading music. Find a curriculum that has solid worship music that teaches kids motions to songs and effectively supplements the story and direction for the day. Evaluate your children's ministry with your children's leaders (including some introspection from them), and figure out what sort of curriculum would best fill in the gaps that your core leadership personalities do not fill.

Curriculum can drive budget decisions. Perhaps there isn't much money to be spent on extra resources like craft supplies, or there is no more room in the church for a craft closet or resource room. Look for a curriculum that has most of the crafts built right in. If money was spent last year to buy a suite of music videos for children's church, worship videos don't need to be a priority in the new curriculum purchase. If there are lots of people supporting the church by replenishing craft supplies, a curriculum heavy on the chenille stems and glitter might be a great choice.

There is plenty of free curriculum out there. Some of it is pretty good. Some of it is bare bones. The highest-quality curricula, though, usually cost money. These are the ones that will resource leaders with everything they need, coming alongside them to be what the leader was not necessarily built to be. If you're looking for a curriculum with teacher training, extra resources, tactile and digital elements, etc., you'll need space in the budget to make this a reality.

Curriculum can be an important element in children's ministry, both in the classroom and the large-group worship setting. Make space to carefully consider your own church's needs and abilities when choosing the right one.

✺ 8 ✺
HIRING A CHILDREN'S LEADER

Maybe you've been reading this book because you are a children's leader in need of some new ways to think about things that are already familiar to you. Maybe you're a church leader outside of the "inner circle" of children's ministry and you've been reading to gain some insider knowledge. Maybe you work with a children's leader every day. If this is the case, this bonus chapter might not be for you. It's a bonus, so you can still tell everyone you read the whole book. No judgment.

Maybe your church doesn't have a children's leader and you'd really like to advocate for that. Maybe you're ready to hire your first children's leader or your next children's leader. If this is you, keep reading. I'll speak specifically to church leaders (lead pastors, executives, etc.) who find themselves in charge of hiring. Let's take a look at some of the big rocks in the children's leader hiring process.

INTROSPECTION

Pastor, finding the right children's leader starts with you. Well, obviously this starts with prayer, but assuming you've been praying about it, you're next on the process list. Asking a question like, "What kind of children's leader am I looking for?" is first about what you expect from them. Let's look at two different types of children's leader. I call them the Jedi and the Padawan. If you're not familiar with Star Wars lore, a Jedi is a master, completely trained and battle-ready. The Padawan is a Jedi's apprentice, showing the foundation for the necessary skills to be a Jedi (in their case, a sensitivity to and ability to use The Force, but I digress) but still needing both mentorship and experience.

1. The Jedi. Are you looking for a complete leader? Are you looking for someone who checks all your boxes, is a strong recruiter, a great preacher, administrative, pastoral, with a solid background in theology and teaching kids? That children's leader exists, to be sure. I know lots of them! They are ready to come in and get started with a ministry plan and action items. These leaders are usually experienced, with several years of ministry experience. They likely have degrees that directly apply to either teaching children (such as elementary education) or pastoring (such as ministry or theology). These are top-drawer children's leaders. Because they are experienced, educated, and probably a little older, they will also likely be in search of a competitive full-time package.

These leaders won't require nearly as much from you. Certainly they will want your partnership, mentorship, and support, but they have the necessary skill set to do the job without you needing to invest significant amounts of your own time into children's ministry. If you don't feel like you're properly equipped to get your hands too dirty in ministry to kids, or if you don't have a lot of extra time to give to it, these are the leaders you want to seek.

☀ **As you consider your options, ask the question, "Do I have the skills to teach a children's leader what they need to know?"**

2. The Padawan. If you're unable to provide a full-time package right now, you might need to look at leaders who don't necessarily check all of your boxes. They might be younger or have less formal education. They might be in the middle of their education. They might not be young, but new to the role of children's ministry leader. There are lots of seminary students, or freshly graduated holders of children's ministry degrees, or second-career adults out there who can be quality children's leaders. I know many of these as well! What they need, though, may require more from you. This is where the introspection comes in.

How much time do you have to give to training and mentorship? Are you feeling stretched thin and want to hire a children's leader who can lighten the load? That's great, but if you're hiring someone from this second group, the Padawans, you need to continue to expect to give extra time. Hiring a younger, less-experienced children's leader and expecting them to check all the boxes with no intentional mentorship is unfair. It's a recipe for double-sided frustration and burnout. If you're hiring a Padawan, expect to invest time into them. If you don't have that extra time to give, hire a Jedi.

As you consider your options, ask the question, "Do I have the skills to teach a children's leader what they need to know?" If you're a lead pastor, executive pastor, or deacon in the church with no background in children's ministry, you can't expect yourself to be the mentor your new children's leader is going to need. You probably have some of the necessary skills. You can offer direction theologically, or you are a strong administrator and can help get processes and systems in place. That's great! What about when your new children's leader is struggling with a preschooler who has major behavioral issues? What about counseling an eight-year-old whose parents recently got divorced? What about articulating your doctrine of sanctification to a preteen? Do you have the training, skill set, and time to invest in these conversations with your new leader? Are you the mentor your leader is going to need? Maybe you are, and you've got the time, and you're ready to hire a Padawan. Maybe you're asking these questions of yourself and realizing this doesn't really describe you. What's the plan to help your new leader be successful, then?

A children's pastor was hired at a church plant out West. This was her first children's pastorate and first position in the church. She was a second-career children's pastor, experiencing a call to ministry after some major life changes in her thirties. She had volunteered in children's ministries for years but had no formal training in child development, education, theology, or ministry. She had obvious skills with kids and adults alike but was in need of continued mentorship. Even though she was a little older than the young seminary students and college grads that get hired into the field, she was still firmly in the Padawan camp when this church reached out.

Her new lead pastor was aware that his new children's pastor was still pretty green. He was also a busy guy, at a church with multiple services and with no particular background in children's ministry. Wisely, though, he recognized he was hiring a Padawan with great potential and she would need some coaching. So he put a plan in place to help her be successful.

His new children's pastor was set up with two different mentor relationships from the beginning of her employment. The first was another staff member who had been involved with children's ministry at the church since the beginning. She functioned in the role of a director and would work side by side, as both colleague and coach, with the new children's pastor. She knew the culture of children's ministry at the church. She knew the people. She knew the way the ministry functioned day-to-day. She became the children's pastor's go-to for any church-related issues, as well as a built-in sounding board as she worked her way through her first year.

The second mentor was an experienced children's pastor at a larger church in the area. The church plant had been experiencing growth and was on an upward trend. The lead pastor recognized how easy it would be for a new children's pastor to come, figure out the systems, and fall easily into the rhythms of weekly ministry. He instead wanted her thinking about growth and change from the very beginning, so he set her up with this mentor to help her think about things from an outsider's perspective, and help her develop ministries in a way that could grow as the church grew. His plan was strategic, and he had the future in mind as he put these relationships in place.

> ☀ **Do you have a strong philosophy of children's ministry to which you'll want your new leader to adhere? Do you want your new leader to come with their own passionate philosophy behind which they can rally the troops? This is something you'll need to establish before you ever begin making phone calls.**

This pastor did the necessary introspective work on the front end to know that he was indeed in a place where he could hire a less experienced children's pastor, a Padawan, because he could develop her through strategic mentorships. He recognized that he wasn't necessarily the one who had the time or skills to make this investment, but he deftly used the skills around him to set everyone up for success.

Further introspection will help as you articulate your church's ministry philosophy. Do you have a strong philosophy of children's ministry to which you'll want your new leader to adhere? Do you want your new leader to come with their own passionate philosophy behind which they can rally the troops? This is something you'll need to establish before you ever begin making phone calls. If you don't have a philosophy that is driving you, you'll want your potential candidates to articulate their own. If you do have one, you'll want your potential candidates to know this early in the process. Chances are, if you have a solid philosophy of ministry you'll want your new leader to adopt, you're likely looking for a Padawan. If you want your new leader to bring a strong philosophy with them, you may be looking for a Jedi.

WHO IS INVOLVED?

As a general rule of hiring, it's wise to include the counsel of those who will be directly affected by the hire. Children's ministry is a little unique in that we as adults are still making decisions for the children in our lives. Therefore, I don't necessarily suggest surveying the kids to find out what they want in a children's leader. We know what they need. They need someone who will love them, who will care about their spiritual, emotional, and social development, who will teach them with a strong theological base, and who will develop relationships with them that keep the kids wanting to come back. However, there may be some specifics you need this children's leader to have. Maybe you're a highly media-driven church and need someone who isn't overwhelmed with all the technology around them. Maybe your church has performed a Christmas musical since 1894 and you need someone who feels comfortable directing it. You may have some core tenets of who you are that are more specific than the broad requirements of a decent children's leader. This is where your extra voices come in.

Hear from parents. Gather a team of core parents who have kids spanning nursery through preteen. These should be parents who are willing to engage in the conversation, not just listen passively. Don't let the group get larger than seven or so, lest you begin to deal with too many voices in the room and an inability to reach consensus on anything. Let your parents help shape the job description of your new children's leader. Shape it, not write it. Your new leader can't be expected to be all things for all people. A group of parents could easily come up with a job description that scratched every specific itch in the room, but it would be a pie in the sky and no children's leader would be able to live up to it. However, listen well as they discuss what's really important to them as parents and allow that to shape your search.

This parent team could even be a stop in the interview process. When I interviewed at one church for a children's pastor position, I went through several interview levels. I met with the executive pastor via video chat. I then met with the executive and lead pastors in person. I then had dinner with them, their wives, and I brought my wife. Then, the executive pastor took me to the home of one of the parents on the search team they had put together. There were several families waiting for us, and we had interview round four where they asked questions about relationships, philosophy, personal ministry goals, etc. It felt very casual, but I was glad to see that the church valued the opinions of their families enough to involve this core group in the process. Your new children's leader will be ministering significantly to these parents. Therefore, involve parents in the search.

The other core group you can benefit by hearing from is volunteers. Again, gather volunteers from nursery through preteen. Chances are, some of these may also be parents from your first group. While your parents know ministry as "customers," your volunteers know it more like "employees." They have insider knowledge to the way children's ministry works on Sundays, Wednesdays, at large events, and at other ongoing ministries. They can talk about specific skills the new children's leader should have. These may be needs of which you were completely unaware. They can tell you what was really working with the last children's leader, or what was really hard. Or, if they're volunteers that have been leading the ministry and you're hiring your first children's leader, they can tell how their time is spent so you can best lay out what weekly ministry looks like at your church for your new leader. Again, your volunteers should not be creating the job description, but they should be helping to shape it.

THE SEARCH

Take a look back through this book to help you develop a lens through which to look for a children's leader. Based on what you've read, here are a few questions you might ask a potential children's pastor.

1. Why does children's ministry matter? Why have you dedicated your life to ministering to kids and families?

2. Your résumé indicates your formal training, but what do you feel is your level of competency in these other areas?

   a. Leadership?

   b. Team building?

   c. Pastoral care and counseling?

3. Children's ministry is not just ministry to kids. You'll be ministering to adult volunteers and parents. What's your comfort level in leading adults? What experience do you have leading adults?

4. How would you hope to grow and strengthen our children's ministry volunteer team? Describe how you've created and organized a volunteer team in the past.

5. How would you define intergenerational ministry? Why is it valuable to you?

6. Keeping kids safe is very important to us. What does a church that is safe for both kids and volunteers look like to you?

7. What do you feel your strengths are? What about your weaknesses? How would you go about supplementing those areas of your ministry?

8. Can you state your philosophy of ministry to kids in a few sentences?

You could also take these and turn them into statements if you're interested in creating a formal job description. This is certainly not exhaustive, because your job description may include expected hours, staff dynamics, and specifics to your church. However, these core competencies can help to shape your job description from a philosophical standpoint. For example:

The children's pastor should have the ability to:

1. Articulate his or her children's ministry philosophy

2. Build and lead teams, offer pastoral care, and lead with competent theology and practical application

3. Lead and minister to parents and adult volunteers

4. Manage a large volunteer core, including recruiting and sustaining

5. Define intergenerational ministry and where it falls in his or her overall plan and philosophy

6. Keep up with modern child safety procedures and train volunteers to do the same

7. Be a lifelong learner, always looking for ways to build his or her skill set

8. Finally, please include your philosophy of ministry to kids with résumé.

OR

_____ is our philosophy of ministry to kids. How does this resonate with you?

If you want to enhance this list, there are many social media pages dedicated to children's ministry. Job openings are posted to them regularly. There are also children's ministry websites and conferences that have job boards available for this kind of search. In my denomination there are specific job boards, as well. This may be the case in your own denomination, so check with your global office about a place to take your search.

Besides these job boards, many Christian universities that have pastoral preparation programs include majors, minors, and certificates in children's ministry and family ministry. Many of these children's ministry degree programs are fairly new, as the phenomenon of the professional children's pastor role is still emerging. If you're looking for a promising Padawan, these universities would be an excellent place to begin.

Blessings in your search for a children's leader! You're investing in a position that can change the trajectory of your church forever. The church of today and the church of tomorrow depend significantly on those called to minister to kids and families, discipling young worshipers and equipping parents to pastor their own kids. Make the most of your opportunity!

NOTES

CHAPTER 1

1. George Barna, *Transforming Children into Spiritual Champions: Why Children Should Be Your Church's #1 Priority* (Ventura, CA: Regal Books, 2003), 34.

2. Catherine Stonehouse, *Joining Children on the Spiritual Journey: Nurturing a Life of Faith* (Grand Rapids: BridgePoint Books, 1998), 21.

3. Dvora Meyers, "Simone Biles' Mental Gymnastics," *Buzzfeed News*, July 8, 2016, https://www.buzzfeed.com/dvorameyers/simone-biles-mental-gymnastics?utm_term=.hnA0MWJo0#.dp0nV021n.

4. Cheri Fuller, *Opening Your Child's Spiritual Windows: Ideas to Nurture Your Child's Relationship with God* (Grand Rapids: Zondervan Publishing House, 2001), 34.

5. Barna, *Transforming Children,* 100-101.

6. James K. A. Smith, *Desiring the Kingdom: Worship, Worldview, and Cultural Formation* (Grand Rapids: Baker, 2009), 18.

7. Lydia Saad, "Sermon Content Is What Appeals Most to Churchgoers," Gallup News, April 14, 2017, http://news.gallup.com/poll/208529/sermon-content-appeals-churchgoers.aspx.

8. Daron Brown, *Shift: How Nine Churches Experienced Vibrant Renewal* (Kansas City, MO: Beacon Hill Press of Kansas City, 2012), 68.

CHAPTER 2

1. Bruce L. Peterson, *Foundations of Pastoral Care* (Kansas City, MO: Beacon Hill Press of Kansas City, 2007), 27.

CHAPTER 3

1. *The Muppet Movie,* directed by James Frawley (Los Angeles: Jim Henson Home Entertainment), DVD.

CHAPTER 5

1. Dr. Steve R. Parr and Dr. Tom Crites, *Why They Stay: Helping Parents and Church Leaders Make Investments That Keep Children and Teens Connected to the Church for a Lifetime* (Bloomington, IN: WestBow Press, 2015), 88.

2. Ibid., 91.

CHAPTER 6

1. Boz Tchividjian, "Startling Statistics: Child sexual abuse and what the church can begin doing about it," Religion News Service, January 9, 2014, http://religionnews.com/2014/01/09/startling-statistics/.

ACKNOWLEDGMENTS

It has been a gift and a challenge to write my very first book. It feels bizarre to take credit for anything written on these pages when there have been so many people who have influenced, encouraged, and shaped me. Thanks to the churches that have called me Pastor. I don't wear that title lightly. I am blessed to answer a calling to serve God's people. Thanks to the other pastors who have served alongside me as colleagues and mentors. You continue to teach me how to learn, how to think, and how to lead. Thanks to Jeremy Bond, my longtime partner in ministry. He reads everything I write, and our relationship is tenured enough that he can just tell me if something is terrible. And thanks to The Foundry Publishing for having the confidence to allow an untested writer the opportunity to pen these words.

www.ingramcontent.com/pod-product-compliance
Lightning Source LLC
LaVergne TN
LVHW051522070426
835507LV00023B/3241